# GRENDEL

*John Gardner*

# INTRODUCTION:
## STOPPING TO BUY SPARKNOTES ON A SNOWY EVENING

Whose words these are you *think* you know.
Your paper's due tomorrow, though;
We're glad to see you stopping here
To get some help before you go.

Lost your course? You'll find it here.
Face tests and essays without fear.
Between the words, good grades at stake:
Get great results throughout the year.

Once school bells caused your heart to quake
As teachers circled each mistake.
Use SparkNotes and no longer weep,
Ace every single test you take.

Yes, books are lovely, dark, and deep,
But only what you grasp you keep,
With hours to go before you sleep,
With hours to go before you sleep.

# CONTENTS

# CONTEXT

JOHN CHAMPLIN GARDNER WAS BORN in Batavia, New York, on July 21, 1933, to John Champlin, a dairy farmer and lay Presbyterian preacher, and Priscilla Gardner, an English teacher. A few months shy of his twelfth birthday, Gardner inadvertently killed his younger brother Gilbert in a gruesome accident, running him over with a heavy farm machine. The incident haunted Gardner for the rest of his life in the form of nightmares and flashbacks, and the deep psychological wound it caused inspired and informed much of Gardner's work, particularly the posthumously published novel *Stillness* (1986).

In his youth, Gardner developed an interest in cartoons and comics, and that medium's fantastic, over-the-top quality pervades his fiction. Gardner often uses grotesque, cartoonish imagery to distance readers emotionally from his characters, so as to avoid overly sentimental interpretations. An avid cartoonist and illustrator himself, Gardner insisted that all of his novels written for the Knopf publishing firm be illustrated. *Grendel* (1971), for example, features the nearly abstract woodcuts of Emil Antonucci, which serve to enhance the novel's surreal, fanciful tone.

Gardner went on to graduate Phi Beta Kappa from Washington University in St. Louis in 1955 and then attended the University of Iowa for graduate study. At Iowa he studied medieval literature and creative writing, eventually combining his two academic interests in his doctoral dissertation, a novel called *The Old Men*. Gardner accepted a teaching position at Oberlin College in Ohio directly after leaving Iowa, and he continued to teach at various universities for the rest of his life. He gained prominence as a teacher of creative writing, particularly at institutions such as the Bread Loaf Writer's Conference in Middlebury, Vermont.

Gardner was a prolific and mercurial writer, producing a remarkable thirty-five volumes in just twenty-five years. The breadth of his output is equally impressive: though most noted for his novels, Gardner also published poetry, plays, short stories, opera librettos, scholarly texts, and children's picture books. Even his novels do not share a coherent, sustained style or tone: they vary from the highly stylized, densely allusive *Grendel* to more traditionally realist works such as *Nickel Mountain* (1973). Critical response to

Gardner's work has been equally divided, and throughout his publishing career the release of a new Gardner work was an occasion for much critical debate. *Grendel* was, in fact, the first and only Gardner volume to receive near-unanimous critical acclaim, though three of his novels—*The Sunlight Dialogues* (1972), *Nickel Mountain,* and *October Light* (1976)—were popular best-sellers.

Gardner's work is often classified as postmodernist. In the early part of the century, writers such as T.S. Eliot, Virginia Woolf, and James Joyce experimented with an idea that came to be known as modernism, characterized by experimentation with new, nontraditional forms of expression. These modernist writers discarded nineteenth-century writers' emphasis on realistic, authoritative narration in favor of a style that was more subjective and impressionistic, focusing more on *how* people look at the world than on what they actually see. As experimentation with modernism developed, boundaries between literary genres began to break down, and writers explored ideas of fragmentation and discontinuity in both subject matter and stylistic form. Modernist pieces often display an acute sense of meta-awareness, meaning they are conscious of their status as artistic works—representations of reality rather than reality itself. Many modernist authors use these techniques to convey a mournful nostalgia for a world they perceive as having passed. Postmodernism, on the other hand, celebrates fragmentation rather than mourning its necessity: postmodern works frequently find liberation and exhilaration in the breakdown of what are seen as outdated, claustrophobic categories.

Though Gardner and his contemporaries—who included William Gass, John Barth, and Donald Barthelme—wrote highly inventive, genre-bending works of literature in the 1970s, Gardner was never a career postmodernist. In fact, he frustrated many critics because of his seemingly arbitrary use of postmodern techniques, which factored heavily in some of his novels but disappeared entirely from others. Critics could never seem to agree whether Gardner was a traditionalist masquerading as an innovator or vice versa. Gardner himself rejected the postmodern label, as he associated it with a school of writers he considered too harsh and cynical.

*Grendel,* one of Gardner's more stylistically and thematically postmodern novels, is an example of a metafiction—fiction about fiction. The plot and characters of the novel come from the sixth-century Anglo-Saxon poem *Beowulf,* a text that Gardner had been teaching at the university level for some time. *Beowulf* is a heroic epic chronicling the illustrious deeds of the great Geatish warrior Beowulf, who voyages across the sea to rid the Danes of a horrible monster, Grendel, who has been terrorizing their kingdom. Gardner's twist on the tale is his choice to narrate the story from the monster's point of view, transforming a snarling, terrible beast into a lonely but intelligent outsider who bears a striking resemblance to his human adversaries. In his retelling of the *Beowulf* story, Gardner comments not only on the Anglo-Saxon civilization and moral code the original poem depicts, but also on the human condition more generally.

Gardner's perhaps most vexing publication is his literary manifesto *On Moral Fiction* (1978), in which the author calls for art that uplifts and celebrates faith, decrying the mass of contemporary literature as too cynical and fatalistic. The book's self-aggrandizing, moralistic tone enraged and inflamed the normally rarefied literary community, and it sparked a nationwide debate that was played out in the popular media. Reviewers attacked not only Gardner's smugness but also what they perceived as shoddy reasoning and messy scholarship. Perhaps the most damaging effect of *On Moral Fiction*'s publication, though, has been the subsequent tendency to read Gardner's own philosophically provocative and complex novels through his straitlaced moral frameworks.

Gardner published several more works after the publicity disaster of *On Moral Fiction,* but, with the possible exception of *Freddy's Book* (1980), none were particularly well received. Gardner died in a motorcycle accident near Susquehanna, Pennsylvania, on September 14, 1982, just days before he was to wed his third wife, Susan Thornton.

# PLOT OVERVIEW

G RENDEL, A LARGE BEARLIKE MONSTER, has spent the last twelve years locked in a war against a band of humans. The main action of *Grendel* takes place in the last year of that war, but the novel skips back in time in order to illuminate the origins of the conflict as well as Grendel's personal history.

As a young monster, Grendel lives with his mother in a cave on the outskirts of human civilization. A foul, wretched creature who long ago abandoned language, Grendel's mother is his only kin or companion. One day, the young Grendel discovers a lake full of fire-snakes and, swimming through it, reaches the human world on the other side. On one of his early explorations he finds himself caught in a tree. A bull and then a band of humans attack Grendel before his mother rescues him.

Grendel becomes fascinated with the world of men, watching from a safe distance as mankind evolves from a nomadic, tribal culture into a feudal system with roads, governments, and militaries. He is alternately befuddled by their actions and disgusted by their wasteful, brute violence. Grendel watches as Hrothgar of the Danes (also known as the Scyldings, after an illustrious ancestor) develops into the most powerful king in the area.

Eventually, Hrothgar's power and fortune attract the services of the Shaper, a court bard who sings glorious tales of Danish kings and heroes. Though the Shaper's songs are only partially based on fact, their imaginative visions of a supremely ordered moral world are incredibly powerful and invigorating. Inspired by the Shaper's words, Hrothgar builds a magnificent meadhall and names it Hart. Even Grendel, who has witnessed the true, savage history of the Danes, finds the Shaper's vision extremely seductive and becomes ashamed at his own brute, bestial nature.

Grendel, increasingly upset by his split feelings about the Shaper, visits a dragon in search of some advice. The dragon belittles the Shaper and declares all moral and philosophical systems pointless and irrelevant. Grendel gradually adopts this worldview and becomes enraged at the humans. He begins to raid Hart systematically, initiating the twelve-year war. In his first battle, Grendel handily defeats Unferth, one of Hrothgar's mightiest thanes (or soldiers), and adds insult to injury by scoffing at Unferth's romantic ideas of heroism.

Other kings increasingly threaten Hrothgar, who preemptively tries to attack one of them: Hygmod, king of the Helmings. In order to avoid a war, Hygmod offers Hrothgar the hand of his sister, Wealtheow, in marriage. Hrothgar accepts, and Wealtheow becomes the much beloved queen of the Scyldings, bringing a new sense of peace and harmony to the vulgar, masculine world of Hart. The lovely queen briefly enraptures Grendel, and only a nighttime attack and a cold, misogynistic look at her genitals rids him of her spell.

Some years later, Hrothgar's brother Halga is killed, and Halga's orphaned son, Hrothulf, comes to live at Hart. Hrothgar and Wealtheow already have two sons of their own, and the presence of so many possible heirs to the Scylding throne makes Wealtheow nervous. Hrothulf, for his part, is disgusted by the split he sees between the laboring class and the aristocracy, and he plans a revolutionary overthrow of the government. Hrothulf's counselor, a peasant named Red Horse, tries to convince Hrothulf that all governments are inherently evil and that a revolution merely replaces one corrupt system with another.

In the winter of the final year of the war, Grendel watches a Scylding religious ceremony. When all the other priests have left, Grendel meets an old, blind priest and pretends to be the supreme Scylding deity, known as the Destroyer. Grendel asks the old priest, Ork, to say what he knows about the Destroyer, and Ork offers him a complex metaphysical system he has spent years working out. Ork is almost moved to a state of ecstasy by the experience, and a puzzled Grendel withdraws as three younger priests come to chastise Ork for his strange behavior. A fourth priest meets them and is overjoyed at the news of Ork's vision.

Later the same winter, the Shaper dies. Grendel experiences an increasing feeling of dread, though he cannot place it or puzzle it out. His mother senses it also, and though she tries warning Grendel, she can only produce the gibberish phrase "Warrovish," which Grendel later deciphers to mean "Beware the fish." Fifteen strangers arrive from over the sea: they are Geats, and their leader is Beowulf, who has come to rid the Scyldings of Grendel. Grendel knows that the Geats are what he has been waiting for, and he is alternately frightened and excited. The Scyldings are none too pleased at Beowulf's arrival, and that night at dinner, Unferth taunts Beowulf for famously having lost a swimming contest. Beowulf coldly responds that Unferth has been misled, and calmly declares that Unferth is doomed to hell because he killed his own brothers.

When the Geats and the Scyldings fall asleep, Grendel attacks Hart. Beowulf manages to surprise Grendel and grabs his arm. As they struggle, Grendel slips on a pool of blood, and Beowulf gains the upper hand. Beowulf begins whispering madly in Grendel's ear. Grendel moves in and out of a series of hallucinations in which he sees Beowulf sprouting an enormous pair of wings. Beowulf smashes Grendel against a wall, cracking his head open and demanding that he "sing of walls." Beowulf manages to rip Grendel's arm off at the shoulder, and Grendel runs off into the night. He finds himself at the edge of a cliff, staring down into its dark, murky depths. A host of animals gather around Grendel, seeming to condemn him, and the novel closes as Grendel whispers to them, "Poor Grendel's had an accident. . . . *So may you all.*"

# CHARACTER LIST

*Grendel*   The protagonist and narrator of the novel. A great, bearlike monster, Grendel is the first of three monsters defeated by the Geatish hero Beowulf in the sixth-century poem *Beowulf*. In *Grendel*, he is a lonely creature who seeks an understanding of the seemingly meaningless world around him. As an outsider, Grendel observes and provides commentary on the human civilization he battles.

*Hrothgar*   King of the Danes. Hrothgar maintains a highly powerful and prosperous kingdom until Grendel begins terrorizing the area. In *Beowulf*, Hrothgar is an exemplary model of kingship, but in *Grendel* he is more flawed and human. Grendel often describes his war with the humans as a personal battle between Hrothgar and himself.

*The Shaper*   A harpist and storyteller in Hrothgar's court. The Shaper provides the Danes with an image of the world as essentially connected and purposeful—an image that Grendel finds incredibly seductive, despite his awareness that the glorious stories of Hrothgar's court are built on a foundation of lies. The Shaper represents the power of art and imagination to create meaning in a meaningless world.

*The dragon*   A great cranky beast that rules over a vast hoard of treasure. The dragon provides a vision of the world as essentially meaningless and empty. Throughout the novel, Grendel frequently finds himself weighing the fatalistic words of the dragon against the beautiful words of the Shaper. Some critics hold that the dragon is not actually a separate character, but rather a personified aspect of Grendel's own mind. Although Grendel only visits the dragon once, he feels its presence throughout the novel.

*Beowulf*   A Geatish hero who comes across the sea to rid the Scyldings of Grendel. Huge and exceedingly strong, Beowulf is cold and mechanical, showing little emotion or personality. In the climactic battle with Grendel, Beowulf appears to sprout wings and speak fire, prompting comparisons to the dragon.

*Grendel's mother*   A foul, wretched being, and Grendel's only apparent family member. Grendel's mother lives with Grendel in a cave in a vast underground realm. She desperately tries to protect Grendel from the humans and his fate. She has either forgotten or never knew how to speak, though at times her gibberish approaches coherent language.

*Unferth*   A Scylding hero who is unable to defeat Grendel in battle. Unferth believes wholeheartedly in the heroic ideals of his warrior culture. When Grendel denies Unferth the opportunity to embody those ideals, he becomes a bitter and broken man.

*Wealtheow*   Hrothgar's wife and queen of the Danes. Originally a Helming princess, Wealtheow represents love, altruism, and an ideal image of womanhood, bringing balance and harmony to her adopted community.

*Hrothulf*   Hrothgar's orphaned nephew. In *Beowulf,* Hrothulf usurps Hrothgar's son as ruler of the Scyldings. In *Grendel,* Hrothulf is a young man who forms ideas of revolution after seeing the aristocratic thanes subjugate the Danish peasants.

*Red Horse*   Hrothulf's mentor and advisor. A crotchety old man, Red Horse believes that all governments are inherently evil and that revolution does nothing but replace one corrupt system with another.

*Ork*    An old, blind, Scylding priest. Ork is a theologian—one who studies the theories behind religion. Mistaking Grendel for the Destroyer, the supreme Scylding deity, Ork describes ultimate wisdom as a vision of a universe in which nothing is lost or wasted. Ork is one of only a few priests in the novel for whom religion is more than an empty show.

*The fourth priest* A younger priest who is overjoyed at the news of Ork's encounter with the Destroyer. The fourth priest has a vision of the universe to which Beowulf alludes in his battle with Grendel.

*The ram* The first creature Grendel encounters in the novel. The ram stands stupidly at the edge of a cliff and will not budge despite Grendel's repeated protests.

*The bull* A bull that discovers Grendel hanging in a tree and attacks him repeatedly. The encounter with the bull is a formative event in Grendel's philosophical development.

*The goat* A goat that climbs a cliff despite Grendel's repeated yells and screams. Grendel tries to bludgeon the goat to death with stones, but it continues to climb.

*Scyld Shefing* The legendary king from whom Hrothgar is descended. In Scyld Shefing's honor, the Danes are sometimes referred to as the Scyldings.

*Freawaru* Hrothgar's teenage daughter. Hrothgar plans to marry Freawaru off to Ingeld in order to avoid a war with the Heathobards.

*The Shaper's assistant* A young man when he first arrives at Hart with the Shaper, the young apprentice takes over the Shaper's duties upon his death.

*Halga* Hrothgar's brother and Hrothulf's father. When Halga is murdered, Hrothulf comes to live with his uncle at Hart.

*Hygmod* King of the Helmings and Wealtheow's brother. Hygmod, a young king who is gaining in power and prominence, presents Hrothgar with a constant military threat.

*Ingeld* King of the Heathobards and an enemy of the Scyldings.

*Hygilac* King of the Geats and Beowulf's lord.

*Ecgtheow* Beowulf's father.

*Finn, Hengest, Hnaef, and Hildeburth* Characters in a song that the Shaper's assistant sings at the Shaper's funeral.

# ANALYSIS OF MAJOR CHARACTERS

## GRENDEL

In the original *Beowulf* epic, Grendel displays nothing but the most primitive human qualities. In *Grendel,* however, he is an intelligent and temperamental monster, capable of rational thought as well as irrational outbursts of emotion. Throughout the novel, the monster Grendel often seems as human as the people he observes. Grendel's history supports this ambiguous characterization. As a descendant of the biblical Cain, he shares a basic lineage with human beings. However, rather than draw Grendel and humankind closer together, this shared history sets them in perpetual enmity. In this regard, *Grendel* recalls the nineteenth-century literary convention—used in novels such as Victor Hugo's *The Hunchback of Notre-Dame* and Mary Shelley's *Frankenstein*—of using monsters to help us examine what it means, by contrast, to be human. Indeed, aside from Grendel's horrible appearance and nasty eating habits, very little actually separates him from humans. Even his extreme brutality is not unique—time and again, Gardner stresses man's inherent violence. Moreover, Grendel's philosophical quest is a very human one, its urgency heightened by his status as an outsider.

The novel follows Grendel through three stages of his life. The first stage is his childhood, which he spends innocently exploring his confined world, untroubled by the outside universe or philosophical questions. Grendel's discovery of the lake of firesnakes and the realm beyond it is his first introduction to the larger world, one full of danger and possibility. As such, crossing the lake is a crucial step for Grendel in his move toward adulthood. The second step—which decisively makes Grendel an adult—occurs when the bull attacks him, prompting him to realize that the world is essentially chaotic, following no pattern and governed by no discernible reason. This realization, in turn, prompts the question that shapes Grendel's adult quest, perhaps the greatest philosophical question of the twentieth century: given a world with no inherent meaning, how should one live his or her life? In the second, adult stage of his life,

Grendel tries to answer this question by observing the human community, which fascinates him because of its ability to make patterns and then impose those patterns on the world, creating a sense that the world follows a coherent, ordered system. The third and final stage of Grendel's life encompasses his fatal battle with Beowulf and the weeks leading up to that battle. The encounter provides, ultimately, a violent resolution to Grendel's quest.

## THE DRAGON

Grendel's encounter with the dragon is one of the most important events of the novel. Cranky and vulgar and undeniably funny, the dragon's characterization draws from sources as diverse as traditional Christian and Asiatic mythology, Lewis Carroll's *Alice in Wonderland*, and the works of J.R.R. Tolkien. The incredible scope of the dragon's knowledge and vision has left him weary and cynical. The dragon perceives the entirety of time and space. Against this vision, man's complete history seems no more than "a swirl in the stream of time." Because nothing man creates—religion, poetry, philosophy, and so on—will survive the destruction of time, the dragon sees all such endeavors as pointless and ridiculous. Grendel senses the essential truth of this statement, but part of him still yearns for just the sort of pursuits the dragon dismisses.

After the encounter with the dragon, Grendel continues to sense the dragon's presence as a smell in the air, particularly when the dragon's fatalistic words are nagging him. We may interpret this lingering presence as a manifestation of the dragon's awesome, omnipotent power; alternatively, some critics take it as a sign that the dragon only exists in Grendel's mind. The fact that Grendel's journey to the dragon appears to be a mental rather than physical voyage seems to support the latter hypothesis.

## THE SHAPER

Throughout *Grendel*, the Shaper and his beautiful though fictional systems are presented as an alternative to the cynical, fatalistic outlook of the dragon. The Shaper represents the power of art and imagination to change people's perceptions about themselves and the world in which they live. When the Shaper first arrives at Hart, he sings a version of history that depicts the Danes as inheritors of a heroic, righteous legacy, all the while downplaying the savage past that Grendel has actually witnessed. Although the Shaper's story is largely fictitious, it enables the Danes to construct comforting, coherent value systems. The Shaper's stories promote heroism, altruism, love, and beauty—all concepts that the Danes come to see as giving meaning to their lives. With these models, the Danes gain a sense that they are striving for something larger and more transcendent than their mundane, individual lives. Although Grendel is fully aware that the Shaper's beautiful songs are built upon a foundation of lies and omissions, he still finds their power incredibly seductive, and he in turn wishes he had something greater to strive for and believe in.

Though the Shaper is an incredibly important and pervasive presence in the novel, Gardner gives him very little characterization. Though the Shaper is often presented as an opponent or counterpoint to a highly colorful character—the dragon—we can find very little to say about the personality of the Shaper himself. We know that he has a mutual though unconsummated affection for a married Danish woman. Furthermore, we receive scattered hints that his attachment to the Danes is built less on a selfless devotion to the community than on personal pride and a promise of monetary gratification. This almost negligible amount of characterization makes us consider the Shaper less a fully realized character than an abstract figure, less an individual poet than a representation of the idea of poetry.

## BEOWULF

In making the transition from the original *Beowulf* epic to the novel *Grendel,* the Geatish hero Beowulf undergoes as radical a transformation as Grendel does. The Beowulf of *Grendel* is uncannily superhuman. He is not only supremely strong, but also a cold, mechanical being who is often described as a walking dead man. This association of Beowulf with death paints him as a kind of resurrected Christ figure. As such, Gardner invites us to read Beowulf's battle with Grendel as potentially an act of bloody salvation. Beowulf is the only being who can inflict pain or physical harm on Grendel, and his horrifically violent treatment of Grendel shocks the latter into a state that is equal parts ecstasy and terror. During the battle, Grendel has a vision of Beowulf sprouting wings and breathing fire. This imagery follows a medieval tradition of depicting both Satan and Christ as dragons. Beowulf arrives as a second kind of dragon at the end of the novel, offering an alternative, total vision of the world and the end of time. However, while the dragon emphasizes the eventual death and decay of all things, Beowulf stresses the rebirth that must always follow. The dragon and Beowulf are further linked because they are the only characters in the novel who actually have dialogues with Grendel.

# Themes, Motifs & Symbols

## Themes

*Themes are the fundamental and often universal ideas explored in a literary work.*

### Art as Falsehood

Throughout the novel, Grendel remains painfully stranded between what he knows to be true and what he wishes were true. From an intellectual standpoint, Grendel understands the world as a brute, mechanical place that follows no meaningful pattern or universal laws. He knows that all the beautiful concepts of which the Shaper sings—heroism, religion, love, beauty, and so on—are merely human projections on the universe's chaos, attempts to shape the world that exists in reality into one that the humans would like to see. The Shaper, for example, tells the Danes stories of their heritage so that the Danes learn to see themselves within a certain moral context. Upon hearing glorious tales of Scyld Shefing, the founder of Hrothgar's line, the Danes begin to see themselves as inheritors of a proud tradition and consequently feel a need to adhere to the strict moral and ethical code that the Shaper has established. The Shaper, in this manner, gives history meaning, cleaning up its messy ambiguities and producing explicit, rigid moral systems in its place. This clear, knowable vision of the world comforts the Danes, who are agreeable to the idea of a world in which kings are kings, warriors are warriors, and virgins are virgins.

Grendel, however, knows that the version of history the epics set forth is essentially a lie, as he has witnessed with his own eyes the truly barbaric evolution of the Danes. Despite his unflagging belief in rational thinking, Grendel still finds himself yearning for the emotional and spiritual fulfillment that the Shaper's beautiful fictions provide. When Grendel first hears the Shaper's song, he is so overcome that he bursts into tears and momentarily loses the ability to speak. Time and again, Grendel's intellect is overcome by the emotional response he has to the Shaper's art. At times, Grendel is even willing to accept the role of the scorned, evil adversary in order to be granted a place in the Shaper's world.

### THE POWER OF STORIES

The power of the Shaper's art and imagination turns Grendel's world upside down, causing Grendel to desire what he knows to be illusory. Grendel finds the epic poems so stirring that he wants to be a part of them, even if it means he must be forever trapped in the role of the villain. On a linguistic level, Grendel is also affected by the narrative he hears the Shaper reciting. When Grendel decides to begin a war with Hrothgar, he triumphantly refers to himself as "Grendel, Ruiner of Meadhalls, Wrecker of Kings!" Even when Grendel glorifies himself, he resorts to the language of the original Anglo-Saxon poet of *Beowulf,* who often refers to characters by such strings of descriptive titles. Perhaps more poignant, when Grendel is chased out of Hart while attempting to join the humans, he expresses his frustration with a stream of human swearwords. Grendel then bitterly observes, "We, the accursed, [do not] even have words for swearing in!" Part of Grendel's frustration with his state is that he must rely on the language of the humans in order to relate his tale.

Grendel is affected not only by stories he hears, but also by stories that exist outside his own experience. Because the events of the epic poem *Beowulf* predetermine the events of the novel *Grendel,* the earlier poem has incredible power over the world of the novel. In *Grendel,* the plotline of *Beowulf* operates like the hand of fate: before we read the first page of the novel, we know that Grendel must necessarily encounter Beowulf and die at Beowulf's hands, for the event is already recorded in the earlier poem. Indeed, Anglo-Saxon culture viewed fate as an immensely powerful force, one that was wholly inescapable. This overarching pattern and plan governing the novel contradicts Grendel's basic assertion that the world is meaningless and follows no set order.

### THE PAIN OF ISOLATION

Grendel's relationship with humans is defined by his intellectual interest in their philosophies, but it is also characterized by his emotional response to the concept of community. Grendel lives in a world in which his attempts at communication are continually frustrated. The animals that surround him are dumb and undignified. His mother not only lacks the capacity for language, but is also dominated by emotional instinct; indeed, we sense that even if she could speak, she would likely be an unworthy conversational partner for the intelligent, inquisitive Grendel. Grendel, then, often finds himself talking to the sky, or the air, and never hears a response. He is largely trapped in a state of one-way communication, an extended interior monologue.

Grendel's most painful rebuffing comes from the humans, who resemble Grendel in many ways. Grendel and the humans share a common language, but the humans' disgust for and fear of Grendel preclude any actual meaningful exchange. Grendel's pain is all the more acute because he is brought so close to mankind and yet always kept at an unbreachable distance. The Shaper's tale of Cain and Abel—the two sons of Adam and Eve who are the ancestors of Grendel and humankind, respectively—further underscores Grendel's tragic status. Grendel and humankind share a common heritage, but this heritage keeps them forever locked in enmity as opposed to bringing them closer. Grendel is just one in a long line of literary monsters whose inner lives resemble those of humans but whose outer appearances keep them from enjoying the comforts of civilization and companionship.

## MOTIFS

*Motifs are recurring structures, contrasts, or literary devices that can help to develop and inform the text's major themes.*

### THE SEASONS

Although the narrative of *Grendel* skips around chronologically, the novel is patterned after the passage of one calendar year. *Grendel* opens in the spring of Grendel's final year of life and ends with his death in the winter of the same year. The seasons are common motifs in literature, with each season having come to symbolize certain archetypes or ideas. Spring, for example, the time when cold weather retreats and new vegetation appears on the earth, has become a traditional symbol for growth and new beginnings—thus making it an appropriate time of year to set the beginning of a tale. Winter, in turn, traditionally has come to symbolize age, maturity, and death. As *Grendel* moves into its final chapters and into winter, the glory of Hart is fading, and the once virile Hrothgar is bowed with age, doubt, and grief.

The period of transition from winter into spring is of particular importance in *Grendel*. This time of year includes aspects of the winter, with its assurance of death, and the spring, with its promise of an eventual rebirth. In the song sung at the Shaper's funeral, we see that this transitional time between winter and spring is the time of year when the Danes gained their freedom from the Frisians, but also the time that brought a tragic queen who ultimately lost her brother and her son. The winter-spring transition is a moment when the Danes regain a sense of freedom, but it also necessarily results in the death of our protagonist, Grendel.

### THE ZODIAC

The seasons are one example of a cycle that takes a year to complete; the zodiac, or astrological system, is another. *Grendel* is split into twelve chapters, each linked with one month of the year and one astrological sign. Gardner includes at least one allusion to each sign within its corresponding chapter. Chapter 1, for example, occurs under the sign of Aries, the Ram, and the ram is the creature with whom we find Grendel arguing as the novel opens. Some chapters feature their astrological signs more prominently than others: the chapters of Aries, Taurus, and Capricorn all feature significant encounters between Grendel and their representative animals. Some chapters and signs require a more interpretive reading. Wealtheow arrives during the month of Libra, the balance; appropriately, we see that she is indeed a force of balance, first between the Scyldings and the Helmings and later within Hart. The zodiac motif appears to have been a late addition to the *Grendel* manuscript, and critics are still divided as to how much weight its symbolism should be given.

### MACHINERY

References to mechanics and machinery abound in *Grendel*. Grendel often uses these metaphors as a way of expressing his frustration with what he sees as pointless, mindless adherence to set patterns of behavior. Grendel sees this tendency in the ram, which instinctually responds to the arrival of spring with a rash of ludicrous behavior. Grendel is especially frustrated when he sees this tendency in himself: he describes himself as "mechanical as anything else" when the warm weather causes him to begin attacking men again. When Grendel is stuck in the tree, both a bull and a band of humans attack him. Once the bull starts attacking Grendel, it never changes its tactics: it fights by a "blind mechanism ages old." Humans, on the other hand, have the ability to make new patterns, to break out of routine and mechanism. This ability is the source of Grendel's lifelong fascination with the human race.

## SYMBOLS

---

*Symbols are objects, characters, figures, or colors used to represent abstract ideas or concepts.*

### THE BULL

Throughout the novel, Grendel condemns animals for the unthinking manner in which they follow patterns. In his view, animals, like machines, pursue tedious routines determined by outside forces (an engineer or programmer in the case of machines, nature and instinct in the case of animals), never making imaginative leaps of their own. The bull that attacks Grendel in the tree is one of the most powerful examples of this unthinking action. The bull, which continues to attack Grendel in the same, ineffective way time and again, comes to represent the world, which similarly acts in a brute, uncalculated manner.

### THE CORPSE

Just before he hears the Shaper describe how he is the descendant of Cain, Grendel stumbles upon the dead body of a Dane who has apparently been murdered by a fellow Scylding. Grendel takes this corpse to represent the essential, inarguable falsehood that lies at the center of the Shaper's myth: the division between human and beast is not as clear-cut as the Shaper would make it seem. Man is just as capable of cruelty and violence as Grendel; it is a lie to say that one of them is cursed while the other is blessed. The dead body represents the burden of the curse that both man and Grendel must bear. However, though Grendel thinks as much about the corpse, he also feels overcome by the beauty of the Shaper's elegant, unambiguous moral system. Grendel stumbles into Hart with the corpse in his hands, yelling "Mercy! Peace!" The corpse expands in significance, becoming not only a symbol of man and Grendel's twinned fate, but also of Grendel's desire to be accepted by the human community with which he has so many similarities. Later, the symbol of the corpse is echoed in the figure of the Danish guard whose head Grendel bites off, signaling the beginning of his twelve-year war with humankind.

## HART

For Hrothgar, his meadhall is a symbol of both his great political power and his altruism. For the Danish community at large, Hart is a symbol of the persistence of their belief: every time Grendel knocks down the door, the Danes tirelessly repair it. The fact that the Danes do so despite Grendel's continued destruction mirrors their unshakable belief in their value systems despite the cruel, chaotic nature of the world at large.

# SUMMARY & ANALYSIS

## CHAPTER 1

SUMMARY

At home in the mere, his underground realm, the monster Grendel watches an old ram stand stupid and inert at the edge of a cliff. Grendel yells at the creature, stamps his feet, and throws stones at it, but the ram refuses to so much as acknowledge Grendel's presence. Grendel lets out a howl so terrible that it freezes the water at his feet, but the ram remains unmoved. The ram's stubborn stolidity reminds Grendel that spring has arrived in a similarly undeniable fashion.

The commencement of the growing season marks the beginning of the twelfth year of Grendel's war with the humans, a conflict he derides as stupid and pointless. Grendel is further disgusted by the fact that the arrival of warm weather has awakened the ram's mindless, animalistic sexual urges. He rhetorically asks the sky why the idiotic animal cannot discover any dignity, but the sky, like the ram, refuses to respond. Grendel responds with an upturned middle finger and a defiant kick. He admits, however, that he himself is no nobler than any of the brainless animals, calling himself a pointless, ridiculous monster who stinks of death. As Grendel walks through his realm, he notices the signs of spring all around him and also notes places where he has committed various acts of violence. Grendel's presence frightens a doe, and he claims the reaction is unfair— he has never done anything to harm a deer.

Passing the sleeping body of his fat, foul mother, Grendel swims through firesnake-infested waters up to the surface of the earth. His seasonal journey up to the world of men is just as mechanical and mindless as the ram's springtime lust, and Grendel laments the necessary repetition. When he reaches the edge of his territory, he stands at the edge of a cliff and stares down into an abyss. He yells into the chasm and is surprised by the volume of his own voice. Grendel continues down the cliffs and through the fens and moors on his way to the meadhall of Hrothgar, king of the Danes. As he makes his way to the meadhall, Grendel thinks of his mother, who continues to sleep in their underground haunt. She is wracked by guilt for some unnamed, secret crime. She has lost the ability to speak, and so is unable—or unwilling—to answer Grendel's questions about the nature of their existence.

Grendel arrives at Hrothgar's meadhall and coldheartedly ravages the human community. This is the twelfth year of Grendel's raids, and he calmly, laughingly anticipates the reactions of the men. They turn off the lights in an attempt to confuse Grendel, but Grendel can see in the dark, and he easily bests the humans. In the chaos that ensues, Grendel sacks up several dead bodies and retreats to the woods, where he eats them and laughs maniacally. When dawn comes, however, the sour meat of the humans sits heavy in his stomach and he is filled with gloom once again.

Grendel listens as the Danes attribute the attack to the whims of an angry god, and he watches as the slow process of rebuilding the meadhall begins. A funeral pyre is erected, and as the corpses burn, the Danes throw golden rings, swords, and helmets onto the fire. The crowd sings a song together, and to Grendel's ears the song seems to be one of triumph. Nauseated and filled with rage, Grendel flees for home.

---

## ANALYSIS

The first few pages of *Grendel* echo the beginning of Geoffrey Chaucer's *Canterbury Tales*, a work that features one of the most famous openings in the English canon. In that fourteenth-century work, the arrival of spring and its fresh, sexual vigor prompts a group of English pilgrims to undertake a long journey to visit the martyr of Canterbury. The presence of the ram is a direct link to Chaucer's poem, for Chaucer's pilgrims are said to set off when the sun is halfway through the cycle of the Ram, or Aries. The poet T.S. Eliot, like Gardner in *Grendel*, parodies Chaucer in the first stanzas of his poem *The Waste Land* (1922). In the poem, Eliot transforms Chaucer's optimistic imagery into a sad and brutal scene, describing spring rising over a desolate, mechanized modern world. Here, in *Grendel*, Gardner appears to be drawing from Eliot's imagery when he has Grendel describe the grasses poking through the ground as "the children of the dead."

We are aware from the start that *Grendel* is a novel whose existence depends on other, earlier texts, not the least of which is the original *Beowulf* epic. The opening of the novel expresses the common tendency in postmodern fiction for a work to call attention to its own literariness—that is, the fact that a novel is actually a novel, written and crafted by an author's imagination as opposed to rising naturally out of the characters' consciousness. It is important to keep in mind, however, that the character Grendel has no way of knowing about the *Canterbury Tales, The Waste Land,* or even *Beowulf.* In some ways, his ignorance of his source materials emphasizes the fact that he is essentially trapped and defined by these earlier works.

Grendel's inability to communicate with the ram foreshadows many of his future interactions. Grendel is perpetually trapped in one-way communications, whether it is with his babbling mother or with the numerous mute, stupid animals he encounters during the novel. The most significant example of this scenario is Grendel's inability to communicate with the humans, even though, ironically, they share a common language. Even Grendel's own mother is either unable or unwilling to communicate with him. Denied any real conversation partner, Grendel is forced to live in an endless interior monologue, with most of his significant conversations taking place within his own head. Lacking any other people with whom to interact, Grendel divides himself into various personas—the sobbing baby, the cold-eyed killer, the raging beast, the charming sycophant, and so on—and thereby manages to create a facsimile of dialogue.

In many ways, Grendel's solitary and isolated position makes him an appropriate narrator for a novel about mankind's philosophical history. Like Shelley's Frankenstein—whom Grendel seems to be aping when he travels down to the Danish meadhall and puts his eye against a crack in the wall—Grendel is an apt commentator on the human condition because he is not invited to be part of it, always remaining an outside observer. However, later in the novel, we may question Grendel's aptitude for the position of commentator, as we see him become more emotionally involved in the lives and dreams of humankind.

SUMMARY & ANALYSIS

# CHAPTER 2

*I understood that the world was nothing. . . . I*
*understood that, finally and absolutely, I alone exist.*
(See QUOTATIONS, p. 61)

## SUMMARY

After establishing the novel's linear plotline in Chapter 1—namely, the twelve-year battle between Grendel and the Danes—Chapter 2 takes us an unspecified number of years into the past to tell the story of Grendel's first exposure to the human world.

In his youth, Grendel explores his vast underground world with childlike abandon. He is always alone, as the only other creatures in the caverns, aside from his mother, are strange, unspeaking beings that watch Grendel's every move but never interact with him. One night, Grendel arrives at a pool of firesnakes. He senses that the snakes are guarding something, and after a moment of hesitation he dives into the pool. When he breaks the surface of the water he finds himself, for the first time, in moonlight. Grendel goes no further the first night, but as time passes he ventures farther and farther out into this strange new world.

Grendel's exploration of the world of humans changes the way he perceives the creatures in his underground world. He realizes that the unspeaking strangers seem to look past him or through him; only his mother truly looks *at* him. She looks at Grendel as if to consume him, and he has an inexplicable understanding that they are connected, possibly even a single entity. At times, however, the intensity of his mother's gaze causes Grendel to suddenly feel separate from her, and at those times he bawls and hurls himself at her. His mother responds by smashing him to her breast as if to make him part of her flesh again. Comforted by this gesture, Grendel can then go back to his exploratory games.

One day, lured out to the upper world by the smell of a newborn calf, Grendel finds himself painfully trapped in a tree. He bellows for his mother, but she does not come. In his pain and desperation, he imagines he sees her shape in a black rock, in a shadow, and in a cave entrance, but each vision turns out to be a cruel tease. A bull appears and, despite Grendel's screams, comes charging at him, its horns ripping Grendel's leg up to the knee. Grendel realizes that the bull has struck too low and will always strike too low; the bull is a creature of blind instinct. Grendel knows that if he can twist his body away, he will be able to avoid the bull's thrusts. This event causes Grendel to experience a revelation that the world is nothing but a chaotic mess of casual, brute violence. Grendel understands that he alone exists, that everything else in the world is merely what he pushes against or what pushes back against him. The bull continues to attack Grendel, but Grendel ceases to pay attention. Nothing seems to matter anymore, and eventually Grendel falls asleep.

Grendel wakes in the darkness to catch his first glimpse of men. Surprisingly, they speak Grendel's own language, though it sounds strange. The men are baffled as to what this strange creature in the oak tree might be. At first they think Grendel is a kind of fungus, but then they decide he must be a tree spirit. They further resolve that the spirit is hungry, that it eats pig, and that they must feed it. Grendel is overjoyed at the prospect of food, and he laughs out loud. The humans take this laugh as a sign that the spirit is angry, and they try to attack Grendel. Grendel tries to communicate with the humans, but they do not understand his words. As Grendel watches them plan their attack, he realizes that the humans are no dull-witted animals, but thinking, pattern-making beings, and therefore more dangerous than any creatures he has thus far encountered. Just as Grendel feels he will fall to the humans, his mother arrives to save him.

Grendel wakes up in his mother's cave. He tries to share his revelation about the nature of existence with her, but she only stares blankly at him. Grendel becomes more and more agitated at his mother's unresponsiveness, and she reacts by rushing to embrace her son. Grendel is sickened with fear, and feels he is suffocating in his mother's mass.

---

## ANALYSIS

When Grendel crosses the physical boundary between the mere and the human world, the movement represents more than a simple geographical change: it also represents Grendel's abandonment of an innocent childhood and the beginning of his new career as a student of human philosophy. Leaving the family home is a rite of passage that we can recognize and understand, an important and necessary step a child makes toward establishing an individual identity. Grendel and his mother also understand this change in a very physical way. As a child, Grendel sees no difference between himself and his mother; they appear to be one entity. When Grendel begins inching out of his home, however, he realizes that he and his mother are, in fact, separate beings. This newly discovered disconnection from his mother frightens Grendel, and his mother soothes him by smashing him into her body, as if to join the two of them back together physically. This gesture reassures Grendel that he and his mother are indeed still connected, and that he is not alone. Afterward, Grendel is comforted and can return to his games again like a little child. The stares of the wordless underground creatures, however, disturb Grendel's simple games and make Grendel highly self-conscious, which in turn reminds him that he is a separate, solitary being.

Grendel's understanding of himself as a disconnected individual is heightened during his encounter with the bull. On one level, Grendel feels alone because no one comes to his aid. His anxiety increases when he looks around and sees nothing but a crazed jumble of images. He thinks that his mother, perhaps, could help him understand what is happening around him. Grendel is no longer a child, though, as he has grown up and separated from his mother, leaving her unable to save him from the confusing mess in which he finds himself. When the bull arrives, however, the world "snap[s] into position" around Grendel. The bull's violent act causes Grendel to understand that his mother can no longer provide meaning in his world—only *he* can.

This moment of sudden awareness marks the beginning of Grendel's career as a solipsist. Solipsism is often defined as the idea that "I am the only mind that exists"—a close echo of Grendel's declaration "I alone exist." We must remember, however, that Grendel is making this assertion while he is under attack by a very real bull—one that shows no sign of being an illusion or a figment of Grendel's imagination. We might, then, come to understand solipsism instead as the premise that "I alone exist *as a producer of meaning.*" Just as meaning earlier emanates from Grendel's mother, now it centers on and is created by Grendel himself. Now he sees the bull not as a thing in and of itself, but merely understands it in its capacity to act against Grendel. This change in perception effectively ends Grendel's childhood and sets him off on his own, adult quest. Now, when he visualizes the eyes of his mother, he knows that he is an "alien" to her, a rock broken free from the wall.

# CHAPTER 3

*Thus I fled, ridiculous hairy creature torn apart by*
*poetry . . . like a two-headed beast, like mixed-up*
*lamb and kid at the tail of a baffled, indifferent ewe.*
(See QUOTATIONS, p. 62)

## SUMMARY

As a preface to telling the story of his war with the Danes, Grendel
recalls the growth and social development of men. In the beginning,
nomadic tribes of men roam the forest. Occasionally, two bands of
men meet in the woods and battle each other, and when they are finished they crawl back to their separate huts and caves and tell wild
stories about what happened. When the bands grow larger, they set-
tle in particular areas and set up large communal halls. The insides
of these buildings are beautifully painted and decorated with tapes-
tries and woodcarvings. The humans plant crops and domesticate
animals; women stay at the camp to tend to home and field while the
men go out each day to hunt. At night, the humans drink and tell
stories about what they plan to do to neighboring halls. Each band
follows a similar pattern of development, and Grendel watches
them all. He is amused by their drunken boasts about conquest, and
believes that they are only partially serious.

One night, however, Grendel finds a hall in ruins, burned to the
ground and sacked of treasure. Grendel watches a change come over
the humans. They enter an age of conflict and warfare. With the
advent of war come war songs that glorify battle heroes and military
events. Goldworkers, who craft exquisite handles for battle-axes,
gain an esteemed place in society. Grendel remembers one such
worker with a cool, superior laugh—"Nyeh heh heh." Confused,
Grendel watches as human warfare escalates and battles gain a kind
of nauseating repetitiveness. He is safe and secluded in his tree, but
he and the humans share a common language. He is somehow
related to these creatures who are capable of such pointless waste.

Grendel watches as King Hrothgar—the same king whose men
attacked him when was hanging in the tree—begins to grow more
powerful than other leaders. Hrothgar is a capable strategist who
understands the principles of organization. Soon, he has neighboring meadhalls swearing allegiance to him and paying him monetary
tributes. Hrothgar and his men begin to build a system of roads,
with Hrothgar's meadhall lying squarely in the middle. The Danes'

military prowess and prestige grows along with their hoard of treasure, which soon overtakes the meadhall and forces the Danes to sleep in the outbuildings. Hrothgar's influence becomes widespread, and Grendel is filled with a murderous unrest.

One night, Grendel watches as a blind old man and his young assistant gain admittance to Hrothgar's meadhall. The man is a Shaper, an Anglo-Saxon court bard. To the music of a harp, the Shaper tells the story of Scyld Shefing, an illustrious ancestor of Hrothgar and the founder of the Scylding (Danish) line. The Shaper sings a generously fabricated version of Danish history. When he finishes, the Danes go wild with glee, infected and uplifted by the Shaper's glorious account of their society and heritage.

Grendel slinks away from the meadhall, strangely affected by the Shaper's magnificent lies. Although he has himself witnessed the true, savage history of the Danes firsthand, the Shaper's account has the feeling of truth merely through the power of its artistic technique. Crying and whimpering, Grendel runs to the top of the cliff wall, where he can see the lights of all the human realms. He screams into the wind, and the sound comes rushing back at him. Grendel screams again and then runs back to the mere on all fours.

---

## ANALYSIS

In this chapter, *Grendel* begins to examine its source material critically. The feudal system and warrior culture—the genesis of which this chapter describes—is, of course, the same Scandinavian society that *Beowulf* takes as its setting. Grendel, however, as an impartial observer, provides a view of this civilization very different from the *Beowulf* poet's. Although *Beowulf* was written by a Christian, English poet some two hundred years after the events it records, the poem still glorifies many of the morals and values its Anglo-Saxon protagonists hold dear. In the poem, the great warrior Beowulf exemplifies the heroic code, which stressed the importance of strength, pride, and valor in battle. In *Grendel*, Gardner parodies that code by showing us its crude, primitive beginnings: two hunters fighting bare-handed in the snow like animals. When these men go back to their camps and tell "wild tales" about their bloody encounters, we see the less than noble foundations of the heroic code, the tendency to record military events in exaggeratedly celebrated song. This chapter parodies the very idea of history that the Anglo-Saxon meadhall culture, with its bards and songs and epics, reveres. Grendel, as a character, is the perfect conduit for such a parody. Like Shelley's Frankenstein before him, Grendel is an outsider. He is a monster , but his resemblance to humanity affords him an objective though distant access to the nature of mankind. Grendel's ability to remain objective is tested as he moves from feelings of detached fascination to empathy and obsession.

When the Shaper arrives, Grendel relinquishes his position in the narrative as the Danes' historian and recorder. Unlike Grendel, who was merely trying to understand humans and make some sense of their culture, the Shaper has a political and social agenda in telling his version of history. His tales of the magnificent Scyld Shefing—lifted straight from the opening of *Beowulf* itself—legitimize Hrothgar's rule, making it appear as if his reign is ordained by heaven itself. The song transforms vulgar soldiers into proud inheritors of a heroic tradition by changing the soldiers' perceptions of themselves.

We can understand why the Danes would be thrilled by such a song, but why do the words also move Grendel so fiercely? Indeed, Grendel has a great deal of knowledge about the true nature of the history of the Danes that should undercut the power of the Shaper's song. The poem offers little by way of factual truth; Grendel's account of Danish history is probably much closer to the mark. Furthermore, Grendel cynically implies that the Shaper does not sing out of any inherent love for the Danes, but merely because he knows that Hrothgar's growing prominence in the area will guarantee him a larger salary. We have seen Grendel begin to develop a capacity for rational, philosophical thought in the previous chapter; the first half of this chapter, with its emphasis on Grendel's detached, almost scientific observation of the humans, seems to continue along that path. The beauty of the Shaper's art, however, completely derails Grendel, sending him back to an animalistic, primal state. Torn between the lures of rational thought and beautiful poetry, Grendel grows confused and panicky. This chapter occurs under the sign of Gemini, the Twins; indeed, the bleating, two-headed beast to which Grendel alludes at the end of the chapter is a fitting symbol of his inner dilemma.

# CHAPTER 4

## SUMMARY

Hrothgar, inspired by the Shaper's song of a glorious meadhall ema-
nating a light that would "shine to the ends of the ragged world,"
decides to build a magnificent meadhall high on a hill to stand as an
eternal testament to the mighty justice of his Danes. Hrothgar plans
to achieve glory by dispensing treasure from his new meadhall, and
he hopes for his descendants to do the same. He sends to far-off
kingdoms for artisans and builders to create the marvelous building.
When it is finished, Hrothgar names the hall Hart and invites all the
races of men to witness it. Grendel scoffs at the pomposity of it all,
but he still manages to get caught up in the joyful celebration and
the endlessly optimistic display of Hrothgar's supposed goodness.
Overcome with grief and shame at his own nasty, bloodthirsty
ways, Grendel slinks away from Hart.

Grendel wanders through the forest, puzzling aloud over the
Shaper's mysterious power. The forest whispers back at him, but he
feels as if a darker, more sinister force were speaking to him as well.
The chilly, invisible presence grows in intensity and continues to
unnerve Grendel. He grabs at a fat, slick vine, thinking it is a snake,
only to discover it is harmless after all. The presence follows Grendel to the edge of town before mysteriously disappearing.

At the outskirts of town, Grendel observes young couples court-
ing. While circling the clearing, he steps on a man whose throat has
been cut and whose clothes have been stolen. Grendel is baffled by
the contrast between the innocent picture of the pairs of lovers and
the violently murdered corpse. Just as Grendel lifts the corpse over
his shoulder, the Shaper begins to play his harp. The Shaper sings of
the creation of the world by the greatest of gods, and of an ancient
feud between two brothers that split the world between darkness
and light. The Shaper claims that Grendel is on the side cursed by
God. The Shaper's words are so powerful that Grendel almost
believes them, although he takes the corpse—a man murdered by his
fellow men—as proof that the notion of a clear divide between man
and monster is flawed. Nonetheless, overcome by the power of the
Shaper's song, Grendel staggers toward the hall with the body in his
hands, crying for mercy and declaring himself a friend. The men do
not understand Grendel's cries, and they chase him out of the town
with battle-axes and poison-tipped spears.

Grendel throws himself down on the forest floor, causing a twelve-foot crack to appear in the ground. He swears at Hrothgar's Danes with curses he has picked up from human conversations he has overheard. When Grendel regains his calm, he looks up through the treetops, half expecting to see the god whom the Shaper described. Grendel asks the sky why he cannot have someone to talk to, as Hrothgar and the Shaper do. Grendel comforts himself with the knowledge that the Danes are doomed: he knows enough about human nature to realize that Hrothgar's descendants are very unlikely to follow Hrothgar's glorious ideas of philanthropy.

Two nights later, however, Grendel returns to hear more of the Shaper's song. Though he is increasingly addicted, he nonetheless is enraged by the Shaper's hopeful words, convinced of the mechanical brutishness of reality. Though Grendel dismisses the Shaper's proposed religious system as a crackpot theory, he admits that he desperately wants to believe in it himself. Once again, Grendel hears sinister whisperings in the darkness, and he can feel the mysterious force pulling at him. He grabs a vine to reassure himself, only to discover this time that the vine really is a snake.

Back in the cave, Grendel's mother whimpers at him, straining for language, but the only sound she manages to produce is the gibberish sound "*Dool-dool! Dool-dool!*" Grendel sleeps, only to wake up to the darkness pulling at him even more inexorably than before. He leaves the cave and walks to the cliff side. Grendel makes his mind a blank and sinks like a stone, down through the earth and sea.

---

## ANALYSIS

The humans' second significant encounter with Grendel links them with him in a new way, scripting a role for the outsider within the humans' burgeoning religious system. The first time the humans see Grendel, they have no idea what to make of him. They run through a list of absurd options before finally deciding that Grendel is some kind of tree spirit. The subsequent battle is marked by a similar state of ridiculous confusion and chaos. However, Grendel senses that these humans are more dangerous creatures than their silly helmets and tiny bodies suggest. They are patternmakers, and therefore far more difficult to defeat than any of the dumb, instinctual animals that Grendel has confronted thus far. Now the Shaper—the most powerful patternmaker of all—has woven a story that not only gives the humans a religious framework within which to live, but also includes a preassigned role for Grendel, who up to this point has been merely an observer.

The Shaper's song about the creation of the world expresses a Judeo-Christian view of the universe, which is appropriate given that the *Beowulf* poet was writing from a similar standpoint. The Shaper's tale—the story of an ancient feud between brothers that results in a world divided between darkness and light—is an allusion to the biblical story of Cain and Abel. The story, found in the book of Genesis, concerns the two sons of Adam and Eve, each of whom brings God a sacrificial offering. When God prefers Abel's gift of lamb meat to Cain's gift of crops, Cain murders Abel in a jealous rage. When God angrily questions Cain as to the whereabouts of his brother, Cain replies, "Am I my brother's keeper?" God curses Cain to wander the earth as a fugitive, but also puts a mark on Cain so that anyone who tries to kill him will be visited with vengeance sevenfold. The idea that Grendel is a descendant of Cain can be traced back to the original *Beowulf* text, which makes the same claim. Furthermore, Gardner's characterization of Grendel's mother early in the novel foreshadows this notion, as Grendel imagines his mother to be haunted by some "unremembered, perhaps ancestral crime."

The role the Shaper assigns to Grendel both pleases and upsets him. On one hand, Grendel takes most of the Shaper's songs with a grain of salt, as he is aware of the songs' fictional quality. Grendel knows that man cannot be as holy as the Shaper suggests, because he himself has seen evidence of humankind's brutality on numerous occasions—if Grendel is cursed, so is man. It takes effort for Grendel to remember these considerations, and finally he breaks down, weeps, and experiences a "conversion"—a word that suggests that Grendel accepts the Shaper's religious vision. To Grendel, the story of God may be a lie, but it is a beautiful one. In this Judeo-Christian system, the outsider Grendel finds a place and a purpose, even though that position is a savage, unsavory one. Grendel is not allowed to join the humans as a brother or a friend, but he can join them, paradoxically, by fighting them.

In this chapter, Grendel becomes more aware of his own use of language, the ways in which it both connects him to humans and separates him from them. Grendel grudgingly depends on man's language as he narrates his story. We see that exposure to the Shaper's song affects Grendel's own narrative style. Furthermore, throughout the novel, Grendel utilizes traditional elements of

Anglo-Saxon poetry, such as alliterative verse and kenning (short, metaphorical descriptions of a person or object: for example, "whale-road" for "sea"). When Grendel tearfully flees Hart after the Danes reject him, he sputters a series of curse words and then laments the fact that even these curses must be borrowed from human language. The great tragic irony, of course, is that Grendel and the humans speak the same language, though the humans are too scared and repulsed to try to understand Grendel when he attempts to communicate with them. Grendel can do many things with language, as his increasing experiments with form and style show; however, he cannot use language for its most basic human purpose—to communicate.

# CHAPTER 5

> [The dragon] shook his head. "My advice to you, my
> violent friend, is to seek out gold and sit on it."
>
> (See QUOTATIONS, p. 63)

SUMMARY

Grendel finds himself in the presence of a huge, red-golden dragon that lives in a cave filled with gold and gems. The dragon has been expecting Grendel, and he takes cruel pleasure in Grendel's fright and discomfort. He laughs obscenely and points out that Grendel's reaction to him is just like the humans' reaction to Grendel. Angered by the dragon's spitefulness, Grendel picks up an emerald to throw at him, but stops at the dragon's sharp words. Grendel, pausing to consider the dragon's comparison between himself and the humans, decides to stop scaring the humans merely for sport. Reading his mind, the dragon scoffs at the idea, asking him brusquely: "Why *not* frighten them?"

The dragon claims to know everything about everything. As a more highly evolved creature than Grendel and the humans, the dragon has a vision of the world that is beyond anything these low creatures can comprehend. The dragon sees both backward and forward in time, though he quickly disabuses Grendel of the notion that this vision gives the dragon any kind of power to change things. The dragon ascertains that Grendel has come seeking answers about the Shaper, and he begins by explaining the flaws in human thinking. Lacking the total vision that the dragon has, humans approximate by gluing isolated facts together and trying to link them into logical chains and rational systems. Every once in a while, the humans sense that their systems are actually nonsense—that is where the Shaper steps in. The Shaper, through the power of his imaginative art, provides the Danes with an illusion that their systems are real. In reality, of course, the Shaper has no broader vision than any other man, and he is still working within the same limited system of facts and observations. His system may be neat and ordered, but it is entirely contrived.

The curmudgeonly dragon launches into a sprawling philosophical discussion, in which he has difficulty making his points understandable to the simple, childlike Grendel. Grendel, for his part, is skeptical about the dragon's conclusions, but he listens anyway. The dragon explains that humans have a tendency to extrapolate theories and grossly generalize from the limited evidence they have, hampered as they are by their restricted vision of the world. The dragon also explains to Grendel how all nature inevitably moves toward more complex forms of organization. He illustrates his point by comparing a vegetable to an animal. If a vegetable is split into many different pieces, nothing changes from piece to piece; its organization of molecules remains consistent throughout its body. An animal, however, has a center of dominant activity—the head—and if that center is severed from the rest of the animal, the entire coordination collapses. The dragon makes the same comparison between a rock and a human. The rock, a less complex object, makes no distinctions about what it attracts gravitationally. Man, on the other hand, organizes, makes selections, and then acts systematically upon his environment.

Grendel and the dragon reach a frustrated impasse. Finally, the dragon reveals that the world Grendel knows is no more than a small ripple in the stream of Time, a gathering of dust that will fade away completely when enough years pass. All of man's monuments, systems, and inventions will eventually fade from the world entirely. Even the dragon himself will be killed someday. In light of this vision, the dragon scoffs at Grendel's attempts to change or improve himself. He grants that Grendel does have a kind of purpose in life: he is man's "brute existent," the enemy against which man will come to define himself. Grendel drives man toward the lofty planes of art, science, and religion, but he is infinitely replaceable in this capacity. Whether Grendel sticks with man, helps the poor, or feeds the hungry is irrelevant in the long run. The dragon, for his part, plans only to count all his money and perhaps sort it out into piles. After ridiculing humankind's theories about God, the dragon gives Grendel a final piece of advice: "seek out gold and sit on it."

ANALYSIS

In the words of the crabby but oddly charismatic dragon, Grendel finds a vision as powerful and provocative as the Shaper's. Indeed, throughout the rest of the novel, the philosophies of the Shaper and the dragon battle against each other within Grendel's mind. In contrast to the ordered worldview of the Shaper, the dragon sees the world as a chaotic, meaningless place, a vision that speaks to the spiritual disconnectedness that Grendel has been experiencing up to this point. The dragon finds the Shaper's efforts to impose meaning on an inherently meaningless world to be ridiculous and small-minded. The meaningful patterns and systems that man creates—history, for example, or religion—are hollow and unfounded. In the face of this all-encompassing vision, the most passionate response the dragon can muster is a crankily resigned cynicism.

In philosophical terms, Grendel's visit with the dragon pushes Grendel's inherent existentialism to the more extreme philosophy of nihilism. Existentialism is a school of thought that presupposes the absence of God and a total lack of meaning in life. As such, existentialism asserts that there are no intrinsic morals or values in the world: man has complete freedom to assert any meaning—or no meaning—as he pleases. Nihilism takes existentialism a step further, to an even bleaker worldview. Like existentialists, nihilists deny the existence of any inherent meaning or value in the world. Under such a system, meaningful distinctions between things are impossible, and therefore all attempts to make such distinctions eventually come to nothing. To the dragon, the values of piety, charity, nobility, and altruism are totally interchangeable irrelevancies. The dragon's notion that the passage of time will erase all evidence of mankind speaks directly to one of the anxieties found in the original *Beowulf* text. As a record of historical acts of bravery, the entire purpose of *Beowulf* is to ensure the fame of its hero and the culture of warriors he represents. For that community, fame acts as a bulwark against the ravages of time. The dragon, however, would reply that fame, too, must fade with time.

Though the dragon is a fully realized character—indeed, the only character besides Beowulf with whom Grendel has any significant dialogue—many critics have proposed that the dragon is not a real being, but comes instead from within Grendel's own psyche. The dragon seems to live in another dimension, one reached not by a physical journey but a mental one, as Grendel has to "make his mind a blank" in order to approach the dragon. Moreover, several characteristics of the dragon are echoes of things Grendel has previously witnessed: the dragon's "nyeh heh heh" laugh, for example, recalls the laugh of the goldworker Grendel once watched at Hart. The dragon is a curious amalgam of dragon imagery from widely varying sources, including Asiatic mythology, Christian texts, and the works of J.R.R. Tolkien, which were enjoying a surge in popularity at the time of *Grendel*'s publication.

Despite the dragon's claims of complete, unlimited knowledge, we should follow Grendel's lead and regard the dragon and his teachings with some amount of skepticism. The dragon hardly bears any of the characteristics one would expect in a sage old teacher. Wheezing, greedy, and slightly effete, he spouts a torrent of philosophical chatter that seems to parody man's own convoluted attempts at making meaning. In fact, the dragon actually quotes a human philosopher extensively in his lecture to Grendel: whole passages are lifted without attribution from Alfred North Whitehead's *Modes of Thought*. The dragon's instruction to "know thyself" is lifted from an inscription at the oracle-shrine in Delphi, Greece. The dragon is more closely linked, though, with the existentialist philosopher Jean-Paul Sartre, a man whose philosophy Gardner often vehemently criticized. In fact, Gardner frequently commented that, aside from *Beowulf*, the second "source" text for *Grendel* is Sartre's *Being and Nothingness*.

# CHAPTER 6

*I had become something, as if born again. . . . I was
Grendel, Ruiner of Meadhalls, Wrecker of Kings!
But also, as never before, I was alone.*
(See QUOTATIONS, p. 64)

## SUMMARY

After his encounter with the dragon, Grendel begins to see the world
as a meaningless place. Despite this new outlook, he still has no intention of systematically terrifying the Danes. One night, Grendel finds
himself watching the meadhall and listening to the Shaper's song.
The song has a different effect on Grendel now: rather than feeling
doubt, distress, loneliness, or shame, he feels anger at the listeners'
ignorance and self-satisfaction. Suddenly, Grendel hears a stick snap,
and he turns to find a guard behind him. The guard strikes at Grendel,
but is mysteriously unable to hurt him. Other Danes rush up to attack
and are similarly thwarted. Grendel slowly realizes that the dragon
has put a charm on him that renders him impervious to weapons.
Laughing grimly, Grendel backs towards the woods, holding a guard
whose head he bites off gleefully.

A few nights later, Grendel launches his first raid on the humans,
thus beginning the twelve-year war. He is filled with joy but,
strangely, also feels more alone than ever before. A few raids later,
Hrothgar's thanes meet Grendel's attack on the meadhall with
much poetic boasting, retaliating with whoops and howls in the
name of Hrothgar. Grendel has a vision of these attacks continuing
mechanically until the end of time, and in his rage he begins to
smash the hall.

From across the hall, a thane named Unferth approaches Grendel. Unferth challenges Grendel very lyrically, and Grendel responds
sarcastically, surprising Unferth with his capacity for language.
Grendel goes on to taunt Unferth about the difficulty of being a hero.
He tells Unferth that he pities the hero's terrible burden—always
having to watch what he says or does, never being allowed to slip up.
But on second thought, Grendel figures, the burdens of heroism are
probably all worth it for the feelings of superiority and comfort of
self-knowledge that come with being a hero. Unferth withers under
Grendel's verbal attack; then, to add insult to injury, Grendel begins
pelting him with apples. Unferth begins to cry, and Grendel leaves
the meadhall with mixed feelings of disgust and satisfaction.

Three days later, Grendel awakes in his cave to find that Unferth has followed him. Though exhausted and battered by his journey through the pool of firesnakes, Unferth nevertheless launches into an impassioned argument that his journey to Grendel's cave will be the subject of Danish songs for generations. Before Unferth finishes, however, he abandons his poetic tone and confronts Grendel about his condemnation of heroism. Unferth claims that heroism is about more than simply fairy tales and poetry. He claims that, as no human will know whether he actually came to Grendel's mere or simply fled like a coward to the hills, his decision to challenge Grendel shows he has inner heroism.

Grendel, however, feels that Unferth has just contradicted his earlier assertion that he will live on in the Scyldings' poetry. Unferth becomes enraged at Grendel's apparent indifference. Unferth claims that heroism gives the world meaning, for a hero sees "value beyond what's possible," thereby fueling the struggle of humanity. Grendel retorts that heroism also breaks up the boredom of life. Further angered, Unferth declares that either he or Grendel will die that night in the cave. Grendel, however, says that he plans to carry Unferth back to the meadhall unscathed. Unferth swears he would rather kill himself, but Grendel points out that such an action would appear rather cowardly. Beaten and spent, Unferth falls asleep on the cave floor, and Grendel carries him back to Hrothgar's hall. Unferth lives throughout the twelve-year war, crazy with frustration at the fact that Grendel taunts him by sparing his life during every raid.

---

## ANALYSIS

Grendel, as he mulls over his meeting with the dragon, begins to display some of the dragon's characteristics: his confusion and frustration with mankind blossom into full-fledged disdain. In light of the dragon's nihilistic views on the essential meaninglessness of all actions and the fatalistic nature of the world, the hope the Danes display enrages Grendel. Whereas the dragon used to manifest himself as a dark, intangible presence in the woods, now he haunts Grendel as a smell in the air, leading him on and goading him into more intense nihilism.

Grendel's engagement with the thanes in outright war marks a new stage in his relationship with humans. The guard who sneaks up on the spying Grendel echoes the dead thane whom Grendel finds behind the meadhall in Chapter 4. In that chapter, when Grendel tries to join the Danes as a friend, he carries the body of the dead thane as a kind of peace offering. The Danes, of course, misconstrue this gesture as a savage display of aggression. Denied a role as friend, Grendel decides to accept the assigned role as enemy. When the Danes approach Grendel this time, he is once again carrying one of their compatriots. In an inversion of the earlier gesture of peace, Grendel bites off the head of the guard—a clear act of war. The experience greatly satisfies Grendel, who calls it a rebirth. Having spent so much time yearning for a place in the world, he feels he has finally *become* something.

We may wonder, though, what exactly Grendel has become, aside from the embodiment of evil that humans have always wanted him to be. When Grendel becomes the "Ruiner of Meadhalls, Wrecker of Kings," he accepts the role of villain and "brute existent" that man requires. When Grendel returns to the meadhall for his first full raid, his presence rouses the Danes. His attacks inspire brave bursts of poetry and zealous attempts to embody the heroic code. Gardner implies that man needs evil or darkness to throw its own virtuous light into higher relief. For now, at least, Grendel is only too happy to be Cain to man's Abel. Even the glorious titles Grendel bestows on himself fail to represent any new identity: they are nothing more than traditional kennings found in Anglo-Saxon poetry. Once again, Grendel must resort to man's terms in order to define himself.

The dragon's charm, which renders Grendel physically invulnerable, is both a blessing and a curse. At first, Grendel rejoices in the feelings of superiority this new power affords him. He enjoys feeling strong and superhuman in front of the creatures who once made him feel confused and ashamed. At the same time, however, Grendel also feels lonelier than ever before. By accepting his role as man's "brute existent," he has finally found a way to engage face-to-face with human beings. Even though Grendel considers man's moral and religious systems hogwash at this point, he nevertheless has—perhaps subconsciously—found a way to experience the kind of connectedness such systems provide their believers. The dragon's charm, however, destroys that sense of connectedness, preventing Grendel from ever fully engaging in his battles with the humans, and ensuring his separation and disconnection from them.

In a shift from the original *Beowulf* poem, the thane Unferth—not Beowulf—represents the traditional Anglo-Saxon heroic code.

Unferth begins his first battle with Grendel like an epic hero, making poetic speeches that exalt his moral code and highlight his bravery in battle. Grendel surprises Unferth and disrupts his performance by speaking right back to him. Grendel undercuts Unferth's attempt at traditional heroism by pelting him with apples and turning the serious battle into a grotesque clown show of sorts. However, though Grendel destroys the trappings of heroism, Unferth later returns to argue for a deeper understanding of heroism. According to Unferth, the allure of heroism is not the fame it ensures or the poetry that it can inspire. Unferth believes in heroism because it gives him something greater for which to strive. Unferth encounters the same problem Grendel does: a vision of the world as essentially meaningless. But while Grendel has decided to deny the possibility of imposing his own meaning on the world, Unferth chooses to use the ideals of heroism to create meaning for himself and all of mankind. For Unferth, the romantic ideal of heroism is a vision, encouraged by the Shaper, that holds existentialism and nihilism at bay.

## CHAPTER 7

### SUMMARY

It is the second year of Grendel's raids on the Danes. The attacks have decimated Hrothgar's dominion. His glory is waning, and other feudal lords are rising up around him. To the east, one such king is extending his circle of power much as Hrothgar once did, plundering neighboring villages and forcing them to swear allegiance to his hall. Hrothgar responds by gathering an army from the farthest reaches of his realm of influence. Grendel watches as these forces gather at Hrothgar's meadhall and grow in number.

One night, when Grendel comes down to spy on the humans, he sees that they have left their campsites. He follows their tracks eastward, to the hall of the young King Hygmod, lord of the Helmings. Hrothgar assembles his troops before Hygmod's door and calls him out. Hygmod appears on the doorstep with six retainers and a great bear on a chain. Hrothgar makes a speech, and it is clear that his troops would easily best Hygmod's in battle. Extraordinarily calm, Hygmod drops his sword at Hrothgar's feet with his left hand—a sign of a truce—and offers him gifts in order to avoid a battle.

Hrothgar refuses the Helmings' treasure, but Hygmod tells him he has a treasure that will change his mind. Hygmod returns to his hall and emerges with his sister, a beautiful woman with long red hair. Hygmod offers her to Hrothgar, telling him that from now on she will be known as Wealtheow, or "holy servant of common good." Grendel finds himself wracked with pain at the sight of Wealtheow; despite himself, she moves him just as the Shaper's song once moved him. Weeping children run up to Wealtheow and snatch the hem of her dress, and Grendel can imagine himself joining them. Hrothgar accepts her as his bride. After a few days of speeches from both the Scyldings and the Helmings, Hrothgar's men return home to Hart.

Throughout the winter, the presence of Wealtheow keeps Grendel from attacking Hrothgar's hall, even though he understands that Wealtheow, in her goodness and selflessness, is no different from any other female creature he has encountered before. Even Grendel's mother, disgusting and wretched as she is, would give her life to lessen his suffering. Sometimes Grendel goes to Hart to watch Wealtheow as she passes the meadbowl around the hall. Her presence seems to have affected all the Danes: the Shaper now sings songs of comfort, beauty, and love, and Hrothgar seems somewhat softened as well. One night, the other thanes taunt Unferth for having killed his brothers, but Wealtheow manages to stop the barrage with a word.

One time during the winter, Hygmod comes to visit Wealtheow, bringing with him a great troop of Helmings. Grendel watches the festivities through a hole in the wall. He notes the doting manner in which Hrothgar watches Wealtheow, and also the cunningly duplicitous looks that Hygmod shoots at Hrothgar. Back in his cave, Grendel is tortured by visions of Wealtheow, which tease him away from the nihilistic truth he has received from the dragon. The next night, Grendel storms the hall and catches Wealtheow up in his hands. He spreads her legs and thinks about cooking the "ugly hole" between them over a fire. But then Grendel, realizing that killing Wealtheow is just as meaningless as not killing her, suddenly releases her. He returns to the mere, happy that his forbearance has surprised the men and wrecked another one of their theories.

SUMMARY & ANALYSIS

---

ANALYSIS

The first few pages of Chapter 7 mark a radical shift in the style in which Grendel narrates his story. Though he has consistently employed a mix of tones and diction, ranging from contemporary swearwords to mock-epic epithets, these pages go even further. The change is noticeable in the shape of the text on the page: beginning in Chapter 7, the text suddenly features italics, parentheses, brackets, and bulleted lists, at times looking more like a film script than a prose novel. The text's expansion into other styles and genres parallels Grendel's own growth as a narrator. As he matures, his language becomes more inventive and experimental. Grendel becomes a Shaper himself. As his linguistic abilities grow, Grendel also becomes more aware of the power of literature and stories. In the previous chapter, Grendel accepts his prescribed role in the *Beowulf* epic. In Chapter 7, however, he comes to understand that he is now bound by that identity: he asks, "What will we call the Hrothgar-Wrecker when Hrothgar has been wrecked?" Grendel now realizes that by fulfilling his goal—destroying the Danes—he will no longer have a purpose in life, thus destroying himself.

The shifting styles, particularly those that appear in parentheses, also illustrate Grendel's constantly shifting and perpetually divided mental state. Although Grendel has visited the dragon and continues to be influenced by the creature, he has not fully accepted the dragon's nihilistic teachings. Grendel is struggling to justify this nihilism against the emotional response he feels toward the lovely, inspiring Wealtheow. Grendel is fully aware of his divided state, and often uses parentheticals to undercut his own words:

> I changed my mind. It would be meaningless, killing her. As meaningless as letting her live. It would be, for me, mere pointless pleasure, an illusion of order for this one frail, foolish, flicker-flash in the long dull fall of eternity.

By framing his philosophical justification as a "quote," Grendel pulls us out of the present moment and forces us to consider the possibility that he does not really mean what he says. Earlier in the chapter, however, Grendel tells us that killing the queen *would* have meaning: it would be "the ultimate act of nihilism." Killing the queen, thereby killing all the love and altruism that she inspires, would mean that Grendel will have finally chosen the dragon—a choice that he is not, at this point, quite ready to make.

Wealtheow, in addition to being an alternative to the dragon (a theme mirrored by the ruling sign of Chapter 7—Libra, the Scales), is the only significant female in the Danish community. Though Wealtheow is awe-inspiring in her beauty and comforting in her kindness, Grendel sees her less as an individual woman and more as representative of the state of all women—as he makes clear when he compares Wealtheow to his own wretched mother and finds little essential difference. In many ways, Wealtheow *is* little more than an epic poet's stock vision of an ideal woman. She performs all the social functions of a proper queen: she is lovely and mannerly, and she brings balance to her community while rarely expressing needs of her own. Wealtheow is never shown with female companions, which underlines her function in this patriarchal society: she exists to articulate relationships between men. From the outset, Wealtheow is a gift from Hygmod to Hrothgar; later, in Hart, she finds herself shuttling among the Scylding thanes, making peace and fostering harmony. Wealtheow is even named in honor of her duty to the men of her world: she is a "servant of common good." Grendel finds this idealized image of women just as seductive as the Danes do, but he breaks that illusion when he storms the hall and exposes Wealtheow's sex organs. To the misogynistic Grendel, Wealtheow's genitals are proof of the ugliness that resides within all women. By concentrating on this terrible image, then, Grendel finds he can resist Wealtheow's temptations.

# CHAPTER 8

## SUMMARY

When Hrothgar's brother, Halga, is murdered, Halga's fourteen-year-old son, Hrothulf, comes to live at Hart. By this time, Hrothgar and Wealtheow have two sons of their own. Hrothulf, though polite, is sullen and withdrawn. Hrothgar tries to attribute the boy's malaise to the trauma of losing his father, but he also suspects that the boy may be plotting against him.

In a soliloquy in the yard, Hrothulf describes the unfair socioeconomic situation he sees in the Scylding community. The peasants labor stupidly for the smug, self-satisfied thanes. Hrothulf wishes the laboring class could view the aristocrats critically and see that the thanes' riches depend on the peasants' labor. Hrothulf describes the system that keeps the two classes apart as a violent one, no more legitimate or just than the violence of savage animals.

In a second soliloquy in the woods, Hrothulf contemplates a large nut tree that provides a home for squirrels and birds, but kills any plants that sprout in its shade. Hrothulf wonders if he should call the tree tyrannical, as only it and its "high-borne guests" survive in its presence. He goes on to compare the tree and the birds to Hrothgar and his thanes. Though Hrothulf has nicer things to say about the kind and loving Wealtheow, simple love is not enough for him to justify the divide between the rich and the poor.

In a soliloquy immediately following, Wealtheow stands above the sleeping Hrothulf and marvels that such sadness can exist in one so young. Wealtheow knows that Hrothulf, though he shows kindness to her sons now, will come to resent them when they ascend to Hrothgar's throne.

A year passes, and Hrothulf becomes even more taciturn and remote. The only times he speaks are on his walks with Red Horse, a deaf and cranky old peasant who acts as his counselor and mentor. One day, as the two are walking in the woods, Red Horse gives the prince advice on the revolution he is planning. First, Red Horse tells Hrothulf that it will be necessary for him to discover ways to frame his revolution—which will necessarily be brutal and violent—as a heroic, meritorious undertaking. Red Horse then goes on to claim, cynically, that the purpose of government is to protect the interests of those who already have power and to deny protection to everyone else. Red Horse also jibes Hrothulf for his revolutionary ideas, claiming that a revolution merely exchanges one tyrannical government for another. All governments, Red Horse claims, are essentially evil.

At a dinner back in Hart, Hrothgar watches Hrothulf sit between his young sons. Hrothgar marvels at the fact that there will come a time when Hrothulf, despite his current outward kindness and lonely awkwardness, will rise against him. Hrothgar scans the crowd before him and sees a series of traps. In addition to the threat that the resentful Hrothulf presents, there is the problem of Wealtheow's brother, Hygmod. Furthermore, Ingeld, the increasingly powerful king of the Heathobards, also poses a threat to Hrothgar's kingdom; Hrothgar plans to marry his elder daughter, Freawaru, off to Ingeld, but he has no guarantee that this measure will stave off an attack. Hrothgar sees Wealtheow as the worst trap of all: the youth she has wasted on an elderly husband reminds him of all the pain and potentially meaningless suffering they have endured together.

Grendel figures that the reader, after seeing Hrothgar in such a pitiful state, must be wondering how Grendel can stand to torment the Danes any further. Grendel responds by claiming that his attacks give men dignity and nobility: he *made* men what they are and, as their creator, has a right to test them. Grendel grows angry with the reader for pestering him with questions, saying that all this grief and energy must eventually lead to something important. Grendel then comes up with a dream that he will "impute" to Hrothgar, about a tree with two joined trunks that gets split by an ax.

---

## ANALYSIS

With the arrival of Hrothulf and his revolutionary ideas, the Scylding community moves into yet another stage of development, with Hrothulf embodying the new era's rising political consciousness. Hrothulf, though young, is perceptive enough to notice the economic and political divide between the haves and the have-nots, and he becomes determined to rectify this imbalance of power. His ideas about the tyranny of the ruling class and the disenfranchisement of the working class are akin to concerns expressed by twentieth-century socialists, who advocated political and economic systems that benefited all of society, not merely aristocrats. In Hrothulf's eyes, the Scylding government has been built on violence and continues to be violent. In the original *Beowulf* epic, Hrothulf actually does usurp Hrothgar's throne; this chapter in *Grendel* gives us the history and psychology behind that revolution.

Hrothulf's development in many ways parallels Grendel's own. Grendel, like Hrothulf, is sad, lonely, and frustrated with the state of the world around him. Isolated and bitter, both characters try to find theories and systems that will fix or explain what they see as the essential problem in their respective worlds. Furthermore, Red Horse's relationship with Hrothulf mirrors the dragon's relationship with Grendel. Both mentors share certain characteristics, such a mocking tone and a superior air. Always a few steps ahead of their students, both Red Horse and the dragon enjoy disabusing their pupils of their idealistic notions. Both teachers take their students' nascent philosophical or political ideas and push them toward the extremes of thought. Grendel, for example, has a general feeling that the world is meaningless; the dragon responds that, yes, the world is meaningless and therefore there is no point in anything. Hrothulf feels that the government is unjust and violent; Red Horse responds that, yes, the government is unjust, but then again, *all* governments are unjust, so there is no point in government at all. Just as the dragon opposes the senselessness of philosophical systems, Red Horse opposes the senselessness of political systems. Red Horse is an anarchist, a person who believes that all governments are violent and are therefore inherently wrong and futile.

Among the Danes, Hrothulf is probably the one who most closely resembles Grendel, which may be why he is the first human in the novel to make an extended speech. Up until this point, Grendel's narrative has mainly been an observation of humans and a record of their interactions. In the last chapter we have seen Grendel become more inventive with his style and form, and in this chapter we see him make another authorial leap. In Chapter 8, Grendel gives us the first glimpse of the other characters' inner thoughts, which up to this point we have likely presumed he has no means of accessing. Whereas in the earlier chapters Grendel watches the other characters as one would watch a pack of animals, now he understands their psychology as well. In fact, there is much evidence to support the claim that all the human dialogue in this chapter is actually created by Grendel himself. Hrothulf's soliloquies in the yard and in the woods, for example, are written in verse. As we may assume that Hrothulf does not naturally burst into poetry, we may infer that Grendel has shaped Hrothulf's thoughts into verse when writing this chapter. Grendel supports this inference by framing a large part of the chapter as a script with scene titles, as if he is writing a play in which Hrothulf, Wealtheow, and Red Horse are merely characters. This is not to say, however, that Grendel is making the entire story of the novel up in his head. Rather, he is learning to structure his story imaginatively, turning his tale into a work of art rather than simply recording events. As Grendel is learning more and more about the power of language, he is becoming more and more like the Shaper.

## CHAPTER 9

### SUMMARY

As winter arrives, an uneasy feeling of dread settles over Grendel. He watches one of Hrothgar's bowmen shoot a deer, and the image sticks with him. Grendel senses that there is a riddle in the image, but he cannot puzzle it out.

Grendel then observes a Scylding religious ceremony spoken in an ancient language closer to Grendel's than to the common Scylding dialect. Images of the Scylding gods are carved in wood and stone and set around the perimeter of a circle. The priests ask their god, whom they call the great Destroyer, to rid them of their enemy, Grendel. Grendel knows, however, that the priests' ceremony is merely a performance, as no one seems to hold much faith in the Destroyer anymore. Once, years ago, Grendel destroyed the religious statues on a whim. He watched the Danes rebuild them painstakingly, and saw that the work, though dull, was somehow necessary to them.

At midnight, Grendel sits in the middle of the ring of statues, thinking of all the Scyldings who are tossing and turning in their agitated attempts to sleep. A blind old priest approaches the ring, and Grendel tricks him into believing that he is the Destroyer. Though Grendel has every intention of murdering the priest, he bides his time and asks the old priest, who is named Ork, what he knows about the Destroyer. Shaken at first, Ork gives Grendel a synopsis of a metaphysical theory he has been working out for years. The Destroyer, the Chief God, sets limitations on mankind, and he is the measure by which the value of all objects is judged. He is the source of man's desire to establish purpose in his life and meaning in his world; God takes care that nothing in the universe is in vain.

The true evil in the world, Ork claims, is nothing as specific or limited as hatred, suffering, or death. The true nature of evil is twofold: first, it is time itself, which causes everything to fade and perish; second, it is the mere fact that one, in being a certain thing, cannot be anything else—thus automatically excluding a host of alternatives. Both of these limitations keep man from understanding the universe as a place where nothing is lost or wasted, which Ork defines as ultimate wisdom.

Ork is so moved by his theories that he begins to cry, and Grendel is so baffled that he cannot decide what to do with the priest. At that moment, three younger priests approach the circle. Grendel hides and watches as they chastise Ork for being up so late and carrying on in such a strange manner. The priests scoff at Ork's idea that the Destroyer has visited him. A fourth priest runs out to join them. This fourth priest is ecstatic at the news of Ork's "vision." Up until this point, the fourth had worried about Ork: he had felt that Ork's tendency towards cold, rational logic was confining his thoughts within a closed system. To the fourth priest, the fantastic vision represents a huge leap in Ork's thought process. The strange vision has caused Ork to believe in something messy, illogical, and ultimately transcendent. Ork is not sure he believes the fourth priest's assertion, though. As the priests carry on, Grendel slinks away.

Grendel stalks the woods, conscious that everyone who was awake at midnight is now sleeping soundly. His senses have grown less acute, and he has a brief vision of the sun as a black revolving sphere covered with spiders. The vision clears instantly, but Grendel is still left with an overwhelming sense of dread.

---

### ANALYSIS

The Danish religious system described in this chapter is poised between a polytheistic system, in which multiple gods are worshipped, and a monotheistic one, in which a single, supreme being is revered. The Danes have a pantheon of gods who are specific and nature-based—a wolf-god, a bull-god, and so on—but they also elevate one deity, the Destroyer, above all others. The tension between these two systems hearkens back to the original *Beowulf* poem, in which a Christian poet wrote about a pagan civilization.

In *Grendel,* religion is losing currency in the Danish kingdom, which provides the old priest Ork an opportunity to come up with a new system. Ork represents a new kind of priest, the only one who has "thought [all the mysteries] out." He is a theologian, one for whom faith and reason are not mutually exclusive. Ork, like the dragon, knows that time will erase everything eventually. In fact, both Ork and the dragon quote from the same philosopher—Alfred North Whitehead (Ork quotes Whitehead's *Science and the Modern World* and *Process and Reality* for his purposes). For Ork, faith in God leads man past a feeling of hopelessness and toward a holy vision of the world as entirely connected, meaningful place. The three younger priests scoff at Ork's radical thinking because they think he is an old, silly man. The fourth priest, however, understands Ork's theology, but he disapproves as well. To the fourth priest, Ork's marriage of faith and reason effectively traps religion within a closed, dead system that holds no place for the absurd, the transcendental, or the truly alive. Though Grendel dismisses the fourth priest's words as the ravings of a drunken man, Beowulf later echoes the priest's words in his deadly battle with Grendel at the end of the novel.

Although *Grendel* jumps back and forth in history, the narrative remains consistently patterned on the passage of the seasons. The novel begins in springtime, a time of rebirth and new possibilities; now, as we move into the final section of the novel, we approach winter, a time of death. This seasonal change foreshadows Grendel's own death, which we know must occur at the end of the novel. The priests, by worshiping a god called the Destroyer, whose sole purpose is to annihilate Grendel, appear to be summoning Beowulf himself. Indeed, the Christian imagery attached to *Beowulf* in the final chapters supports this association. Grendel can sense death's approach—he imagines he hears footsteps and he is afraid. The whole world, in fact, seems primed for some kind of cataclysmic event. The Danes are restless and apprehensive, unable to fall asleep in their beds. Grendel's glimpse of a bowman shooting a hart—a male deer—is a seemingly ordinary event that nonetheless holds great portent, if only Grendel were able to puzzle out what it meant. The world has always been a mysterious place for Grendel, but now we see those mysteries gaining urgency.

Grendel's encounter with Ork and the other priests can be seen as the ending of the second major section of *Grendel*. The first part can loosely be defined as the establishment of Grendel's history and his quest—his endeavor to discover how he should live his life in a meaningless world. In the second part of the novel Grendel finds two very different ways of answering that question. The Shaper, on one hand, proposes that one should make his *own* meaning in the world, and he uses the power of his imagination to create systems like heroism, altruism, and nobility. The dragon, on the other hand, claims that such system-making is pointless and irrelevant, as everything will turn to dust eventually. Characters such as Wealtheow, Unferth, Hrothulf, Red Horse, and Ork provide Grendel with slightly different views on this essential debate. The chapters that feature these characters deepen our understanding of Grendel's dilemma, but they do not do much to advance the plot. The strange stirrings in the winter air in this chapter, however, suggest that we are moving into a new phase of the novel.

## CHAPTER 10

### SUMMARY

Grendel watches a great horned goat attempt to ascend the cliffside toward the mere. Angered by the goat's dogged pursuit, Grendel yells at the creature. When the goat does not respond, Grendel reacts by throwing trees and stones at it. The goat continues to climb even after its skull has been split, and appears to continue climbing even after it dies.

That evening, Grendel goes to watch the humans and their daily routines. An old woman tells a group of children about a giant with the strength of thirty thanes who will come across the sea someday.

Later that same night, Grendel watches as people gather at the bedside of the ailing Shaper. The Shaper tries to make a prediction about the fate of the Danes, but he dies before he can finish the sentence. About an hour later, the news of the Shaper's death arrives at the house of a sleeping nobleman, whose middle-aged wife seems to have shared an unspoken, unconsummated love with the Shaper. Grendel watches old women prepare the Shaper for burial, and then he returns home to the mere.

Back in the cave, Grendel's mother is progressing further and further into insanity. Sensing some impending doom, she tries to prevent Grendel from leaving the safety of the cave. She struggles to speak her fears, but the only thing she can say besides her usual "Dool-dool" is the nonsense phrase "Warovvish." Despite his mother's protests, Grendel decides to attend the Shaper's funeral.

At the funeral, the Shaper's assistant, now a grown man, takes the Shaper's harp to sing a song of a king named Finn, who battles with the Danes, his wife's kinsmen. Finn's troops are decimated in the battle, and King Hnaef of the Danes—the brother of Finn's wife—is killed. Finn and the Danes make a truce, and Finn becomes lord of the Danes. Hengest, a Danish thane, resents Finn and misses his home. As soon as winter turns to spring, Hengest leads his men into battle against Finn. Finn is killed, and Hengest, the queen, and the Danes sail back to Denmark. After the Shaper's assistant finishes the song, the funeral pyre is lit, and the Shaper's body is burnt.

That night, Grendel awakens suddenly and thinks he hears the goat climbing up the cliff wall. His mother continues to make unintelligible sounds, and Grendel deciphers "Warovvish" to mean "Beware the fish." Grendel is filled once again with a vague foreboding. He makes reference to another monster he has met in the woods, a wild old woman. He smells the dragon and finally decides to sleep, leaving his war for the springtime, as is his custom. Grendel wakes a final time in terror, imagining hands on his throat.

---

## ANALYSIS

Grendel's vague feelings of foreboding and anticipation intensify greatly in this chapter, while Grendel tries even harder to stamp them down. He appears to be receiving messages from the world around him. Some of these messages are blatant, like his mother's ravings and the old woman's pronouncement; some are more cryptic, like the goat's mindless climb and the death of the Shaper. Everything around Grendel has become stale, dull and tedious. Despite his assertion that "there is nothing to expect," he still finds himself awaiting a major change. The first step in that process of change is the death of the extremely influential Shaper. The Shaper's passing not only ends an epoch for Grendel but also the very notion of history itself. The Shaper organizes historical detail in such a way that it gives meaning to the present moment. The Shaper's glorification of Hrothgar's ancestors, for example, legitimizes Hrothgar's own rule. In his claim that Grendel is descended from Cain, the world's first murderer, the Shaper employs a notion of history and lineage to justify Grendel's extermination. Upon the Shaper's death, Grendel finds that history has lost all its meaning. Events that occurred in the past stay in the past: neither the glorious deeds of Scyld Shefing nor Grendel's own atrocities exists in the present moment.

The story of King Finn, Hengest, and the Danes, sung by the assistant at the Shaper's funeral, is also sung in the *Beowulf* poem. The original *Beowulf* poet acquired the tale from another, unnamed Anglo-Saxon poem, the only remaining piece of which is known as the Finnesburgh Fragment. In *Beowulf,* the Danes' *scop,* or bard, sings the song in celebration of Grendel's destruction. The tragic fate of the song's Queen Hildeburh—the wife of King Finn—foreshadows the ill-fated alliance of Freawaru and King Ingeld, leader of the rival Heathobard clan. Gardner alludes to this alliance in the next chapter, but only in passing. The true significance of the song lies in the section that Gardner actually chooses to quote, in which Hengest—who took over the Danish troops after the death of Hnaef—decides to enact revenge upon the Frisians rather than return to Denmark. Hengest has spent the winter stewing in his hate for King Finn. The coming of the spring brings freedom to Hengest and a decisive victory for the Danish people over their enemies. *Grendel,* in its journey through the calendrical year, is approaching the same season. The defeat of Finn at the end of the winter anticipates Grendel's defeat at the same time of year. That the song is sung at Grendel's death in *Beowulf* reinforces this association. Paradoxically, Spring has become a time that holds the promise of both life *and* death.

Grendel's encounter with the goat echoes his encounter with the ram at the very beginning of the novel. The earlier scene is broadly comic, as Gardner surprises us by having Grendel, a fourth-century beast, use very foul modern language. The ram, meanwhile, is a drooling, idiotic animal that would be right at home in a cartoon—

indeed, on numerous occasions, Gardner cited the influence of cartoons on his work. Grendel yells at the ram and, receiving no response, goes on his way, grumbling and cursing the stupidity of animals. Here, the encounter with the goat shares many of the same contours as the incident with the ram. Grendel stands at the top of the cliff wall and spies a mindless animal that he tries to shoo away. The slightly vulgar comedy of the first incident, however, turns into something much more violently grotesque. The violence remains cartoonish and over-the-top, but the image of the goat's broken skull is genuinely disconcerting. Earlier, with the ram, Grendel is able to dismiss the animal and walk away. Now, however, something won't let Grendel leave the goat alone, and he becomes obsessed with stopping it. While Grendel attributes the ram's single-mindedness to stupidity, the goat's single-mindedness frightens Grendel with its more sinisterly mechanical pursuit. The goat upsets Grendel because it represents the inexorable approach of death and because it causes Grendel to see his own pointless, self-destructive path mirrored in the goat's interminable climb.

## CHAPTER 11

### SUMMARY

Fifteen strangers arrive in the area by sea, filling Grendel with wild exhilaration. The strangers appear to be the fulfillment of his earlier premonitions; indeed, Grendel feels the strangers' approach before he sees them. A Danish coastguard greets the strangers, whom Grendel describes as mechanical and dead looking. Their leader, a huge but oddly soft-spoken man named Beowulf, tells the coastguard that he and the other strangers are Geats, from the kingdom of King Hygilac. (The leader's name is never explicitly mentioned in the text of *Grendel,* but he is clearly Beowulf.) Beowulf says that he has advice for Hrothgar, so the coastguard points him toward the meadhall. Grendel becomes fixated on Beowulf's mouth, which seems to move independent of the words he speaks, as if his body were some kind of disguise. Grendel watches as the Geats travel like a huge machine up to Hart.

Back in his cave, Grendel is filled with an excitement he cannot describe. He is ecstatic about the arrival of the Geats, and everything around him suddenly seems absurd and surreal. He is overjoyed at the prospect of being released from his boredom, which he describes as the worst pain possible. Grendel dismisses the notion of order, calling it a mere mask that men use to connect the two realities they know—the self and the world. He believes that these theories are just talk, and can be demolished by an act of violent truth.

At Hart, there is an uneasy tension between the Geats and the Scyldings, who resent the fact that they need the Geats' help. Unferth taunts Beowulf about a swimming contest he once lost to Breca, a childhood friend. Calmly, Beowulf explains that he actually *did* triumph over Breca, but that he had to single-handedly defeat a pack of sea monsters during the contest. Then, just as calmly, Beowulf tells Unferth that he will be condemned to hell in the afterlife for having murdered his brothers. The Scyldings are struck by Beowulf's sharp words, and Grendel concludes that Beowulf is insane. Hrothgar deflates the situation by enlisting Wealtheow to serve mead. Grendel once again notices the strange disconnection between Beowulf's mouth and his words. Unferth leaves the hall fighting back tears.

Hrothgar makes speeches and tells Beowulf how he plans to marry Freawaru off to Ingeld, king of the Heathobards. Hrothgar says that Beowulf is like a son to him, which makes Wealtheow—with an eye on Hrothulf—nervous. Beowulf smiles, but remains remote. At the end of the night, as the hearth dies, the Shaper's assistant sings a song about spring overcoming winter. The Scyldings and the Geats go to sleep, and silence falls over Hart. When darkness falls, Grendel decides that "it is time."

## ANALYSIS

In this chapter, Grendel uses mechanical imagery to describe Beowulf—perhaps the most significant instance of the many mechanical images and characterizations that appear throughout the novel. In Chapter 1, Grendel describes the cycle of the seasons as the "cold mechanics of the stars," a chilly and unfeeling progression that locks him into a mindless, endless loop. Grendel also meets three stupid animals—the ram, the bull, and the goat—whose foolish adherence to a set pattern of behavior elicits Grendel's derision and more comparisons to unthinking machines. Machines are a decidedly anachronistic metaphor for a fourth-century monster, but as Grendel is really a modern creature at heart it seems an appropriate choice. The machine is a brute, unthinking creature with no hope of evolving, which Grendel fears is his own fate. Several times in the text he berates himself for being "as mechanical as anything else." We see his extreme frustration at this state expressed in his encounter with the goat, which most vividly and grotesquely represents the plight of the machine. At times, however, Grendel uses the image of a machine to his advantage, presenting it as an excuse for his own violent, mindless behavior. Grendel is attracted to humans partly because they contrast so sharply with the other creatures he encounters. While the bull gores Grendel repeatedly without ever varying his tactics, humans are able to make their own patterns. Rather than blindly follow a system set by a higher power, men are able to assert their own systems of meaning.

The choice to describe Beowulf as a machine, then, is a bit puzzling. Though the human beings in *Grendel* may be silly, absurd, or even one-dimensionally allegorical, they are all real humans with real flaws and limitations. Beowulf, on the other hand, comes across as fantastic and supernatural, almost like a science-fiction android. He never blinks, and when he speaks, his words do not seem to match the movements of his mouth, as if his body were merely a shell or a disguise. Grendel describes the workings of Beowulf's brain as "stone-cold, grinding like a millwheel." On one hand, associating Beowulf with machines causes us to cast a critical eye on his character. Like so many other aspects of the original *Beowulf* poem, perhaps we are meant to question Beowulf's heroism, to ask ourselves whether the unchallenged admiration he is granted in *Beowulf* is truly deserved. Furthermore, Beowulf's machinelike appearance is also ironically appropriate, as it means that the very thing Grendel rails against throughout the novel is what finally causes his downfall.

Beowulf is not simply described as a machine; he is described as a dead man. His voice is that of a "dead thing," and his patience rivals that of a "grave-mound." These images reinforce the idea that Beowulf will be the agent of Grendel's demise. However, as a man who has risen from the dead, Beowulf also resembles the resurrected Christ. Grendel's mother tries to warn her son of his impending doom by bleating "Beware the fish"—fish being a commonly recognized symbol for the Christ figure. Indeed, Beowulf is associated with fish images several times throughout this chapter. He comes from over the sea, "has no more beard than a fish," and has shoulders as "sleek as the belly of a shark." Furthermore, the story of the swimming contest with Breca demonstrates Beowulf's prowess in the water. Beowulf does appear to be the fulfillment of the Scyldings' prayers for a Destroyer to come and rid them of Grendel.

# CHAPTER 12

*It's coming, my brother. . . . Though you murder the*
*world, transmogrify life into I and it, strong searching*
*roots will crack your cave and rain will cleanse it: The*
*world will burn green, sperm build again.*

(See QUOTATIONS, p. 65)

## SUMMARY

That night, filled with excitement, lust, joy, and fear, Grendel raids
the meadhall. He bursts through the heavy front door to discover all
the men asleep. Madly prankish, he ties a tablecloth around his neck
like a napkin and proceeds to eat one sleeping man. Grendel grabs
another man by the wrist, only to discover that it is Beowulf, who
has been silently watching him in order to see how he operates. With
a stare as intense as his grip, Beowulf twists Grendel's arm around in
the socket, causing him pain unlike any he has ever felt. Grendel has
a surreal, fantastic vision of the meadhall coming to life, and he sees
a pair of wings sprouting from Beowulf's back. Reminding himself
that Beowulf is only a man, Grendel tries to regain his senses and
plan a logical attack. But just then Grendel slips on a puddle of
blood, and the accident allows Beowulf to take the upper hand.

Beowulf starts whispering madly in Grendel's ear. Though Grendel tries to avoid listening, he is helpless. Beowulf begins by quoting
the dragon's description of the world as a meaningless swirl of dust.
Laughing and spitting flames, Beowulf speaks of an approaching
period of regeneration in the world. Grendel refuses to be taken in
by Beowulf's words, which remind him of all the talk he has already
heard. Slipping in and out of his visions, Grendel whimpers and
bawls for his mother. He claims that Beowulf has gained the upper
hand merely by taking advantage of an accident: if Grendel had not
slipped on the blood, he would be winning. Beowulf hurls Grendel
against a table and then a wall, demanding that Grendel observe the
hardness of the wall. He continues to smash Grendel against the
walls, breaking his forehead open. Then Beowulf demands that
Grendel "sing of walls." After some resistance, Grendel sings a
short verse about man's walls crumbling with the passage of time,
leaving nothing but the shining memory of the town.

Grendel continues to insist that Beowulf is insane, and that his
victory is only an accident and no proof of the truth of his words.
Grendel is amazed when Beowulf manages to rip his arm off at the

shoulder. Suddenly realizing that he will die, Grendel stumbles out of the hall and into the darkness of the night. The outlines of everything around him appear remarkably distinct. Grendel calls for his mother one last time. He finds himself standing at the edge of the same cliff where he stood in Chapter 1, staring down into its bottomless depths. Something inside Grendel moves him to tumble down into the abyss voluntarily. His sight clears for a moment, and no longer in pain, he notices that his old enemies, the animals, have gathered around him to watch him die. Overcome by both terror and joy, Grendel whispers to them, "Poor Grendel's had an accident. . . . *So may you all.*"

---

## ANALYSIS

In the midst of the climactic battle, Grendel has a hallucination of Beowulf sprouting wings and spitting flames like a dragon. Indeed, Grendel's encounter with Beowulf in many ways parallels his earlier encounter with the dragon. Grendel senses the dragon several chapters before he actually meets him or even apprehends his nature. Similarly, Grendel feels Beowulf's imminent presence long before the warrior actually arrives in Denmark. Furthermore, just as it is unclear whether the dragon is a separate, distinct creature or a creation of Grendel's own mind, Beowulf's appearance shifts and mutates drastically throughout his battle with Grendel, leaving us to wonder if these changes are actually occurring or are merely a function of Grendel's imagination and perception. As there is no logical reason why Beowulf would have such uncanny insight into Grendel's thoughts and psychology, there is a sense that this vision of a dragon-like Beowulf is a private revelation intended only for Grendel.

Beowulf and the dragon are the only characters who speak directly to Grendel and pierce through his isolation, and their messages are closely related, though essentially opposed. Beowulf begins his lecture to Grendel by quoting the dragon, describing the present moment as a "temporary gathering of bits, a few random specks, a cloud." Beowulf accepts the dragon's explanation of the world as a place where everything eventually dies. However, while the dragon emphasizes death and decay, Beowulf looks beyond the moment of death and emphasizes the rebirth that always follows. Beowulf's promise of a burning, avenging spring season echoes the song sung at the Shaper's funeral, which also describes a violent seasonal shift that paradoxically holds the promise of both life and death. Gardner claimed that he based the dragon imagery in *Grendel* on a medieval tradition in which both Christ and the devil were portrayed as dragons. Beowulf, in his association with the dead and risen Christ, also represents the coexistence of life and death in one figure.

This notion of paradox resurfaces in the final moments of the novel, when the one-armed Grendel stands at the edge of the cliff and cannot discern whether it is joy or terror he feels. Grendel's death is clearly gruesome and violent, and we may find his plight pathetic and heart-wrenching. His final words appear to be a curse directed at the mindless, stupid animals that have gathered to watch him die. However, some critics have also interpreted Grendel's final words as a strange sort of blessing. Although in intense pain, Grendel is now free from the mindless, mechanical cycle in which he earlier found himself trapped. Importantly, the impetus for Grendel's sudden freedom from this cycle is a mere accident, his slipping on a pool of blood during the battle with Beowulf. As this twist implies that machines have no place for the accidental or unexpected, perhaps Grendel is wishing an "accident" on the animals as a means of freeing them from their blindly predetermined paths.

The idea of the accident as an agent of salvation recalls the exchange between Ork and the fourth priest after Ork's conversation with Grendel. The fourth priest worries that Ork's tendency to think in neat, closed systems of rational thought is crippling Ork. Allowing himself to stumble into a rapturous vision of the Destroyer, however, opens Ork up to fantastic, absurd, illogical possibilities. To the fourth priest, these illogical possibilities are the stuff of life. Like blood and sperm—two fluids that hold the essence of life itself—truth is messy, explosive, and unplanned. In other words, the fourth priest believes that truth is found in the accidental. Beowulf alludes to the fourth priest's outburst when he describes how spring will burst through the dead structures of winter and "the world will burn green, sperm build again." Grendel, for his part, understands the distinction between "chilly intellect" and "hot imagination," but he refuses to admit that Beowulf might be right until the very end, when he himself concedes to feelings of ambivalence. Significantly, *Grendel* ends before we actually see Grendel take the plunge into the abyss. Instead, Grendel remains poised on the edge of the cliff—an image forever unresolved.

# IMPORTANT QUOTATIONS EXPLAINED

1.  I understood that the world was nothing: a mechanical chaos of casual, brute enmity on which we stupidly impose our hopes and fears. I understood that, finally and absolutely, I alone exist. All the rest, I saw, is merely what pushes me, or what I push against, blindly—as blindly as all that is not myself pushes back.

Grendel has this revelation while the bull attaks him in Chapter 2. The bull assails Grendel mindlessly, never changing its tactics even though it is getting nowhere with its assault. Grendel suddenly realizes that the world is just like the bull—mindless and destructive without any discernible plan or reason. Any attempt to determine such a plan or pattern in the world is a misguided effort, reflecting more the desire of the seeker to find such a pattern than the actual existence of such a pattern. Grendel's revelation has a second component as well, which he phrases as "I alone exist." Clearly, as Grendel is undergoing a brutal attack as he makes this assertion, he does not literally mean that everything else in the world is just an airy figment of his imagination. Rather, it is, for Grendel, a means to organize the way he perceives the world. While he once saw the world as a frightening mass of images, now he can separate the world into categories—namely, Grendel and not-Grendel.

This revelation marks the transition between Grendel's innocent, ignorant childhood and his adulthood as a student of philosophy. Having come to understand the world as a pitiless chaos that fails to provide a moral code or ethical system to guide his actions, he begins to question how he should live his life. This moment also marks a transition into adulthood in the sense that it causes a split between Grendel and his mother. Earlier, Grendel has understood himself as part of his mother, not as an individual being in his own right. When he is stuck in the tree, he looks for his mother to emerge from the shadows around him. If he sees her, then he believes the madness and confusion he sees will return to a sense of order. Grendel's mother never arrives, however, forcing Grendel to accept the responsibility of creating order himself.

2.      Thus I fled, ridiculous hairy creature torn apart by
        poetry—crawling, whimpering, streaming tears,
        across the world like a two-headed beast, like mixed-
        up lamb and kid at the tail of a baffled, indifferent
        ewe—and I gnashed my teeth and clutched the sides of
        my head as if to heal the split, but I couldn't.

Here, at the end of Chapter 3, Grendel reacts to hearing the Shaper's song for the first time. The lines—directly quoted from the opening of *Beowulf*—divide Grendel into two halves. This split Grendel, clutching his head in mental agony, foreshadows the division he later feels when he attempts to reconcile the opposing views of the Shaper and the dragon. The Shaper and the dragon inspire very different reactions in Grendel: the Shaper inspires incredible emotion, while the dragon appeals to Grendel's rational mind and logical reasoning. The portrayal in this passage of Grendel as a beastlike, barely verbal fiend comes straight out of *Beowulf,* and it contrasts with the articulate, self-aware creature we have seen thus far. The Shaper's ability to immediately transform Grendel suggests the power that the *Beowulf* story, as told by the humans, will have over Grendel's life in the future. Grendel, before even hearing what part he will play in these human stories, has internalized the role the humans ascribe to him, turning into the crazed, instinctual beast they expect him to be. By comparing himself to several bleating, dumb animals, Grendel applies to himself the same criticism that he has previously directed at the mindless animals of the forest.

QUOTATIONS

3.   "Nevertheless, something will come of all this," I said.
      "Nothing," he said. "A brief pulsation in the black
   hole of eternity. My advice to you—"
      "Wait and see," I said.
      He shook his head. "My advice to you, my violent
   friend, is to seek out gold and sit on it."

These lines are the final exchange between Grendel and the dragon
at the end of Chapter 5. Though this is the end of the direct
encounter between Grendel and the dragon, the dragon continues
loom over Grendel's life throughout the rest of the novel. The
dragon provides Grendel with a glimpse of the true nature of time,
which the dragon is able to see stretching out toward both its
beginning and its end. The dragon claims that time is like a black
hole, eventually destroying everything in the universe. In the vast
span of time, the entirety of mankind's history registers little more
than a brief flash. The dragon, with this immense, cosmic vision,
can see little point in religion, poetry, or any of the other things that
humankind invents in order to make its short stay in the universe
more meaningful and significant. Grendel understands the dragon's
point on an intellectual level—it is, after all, a philosophy he has
been more or less moving towards since his encounter with the
bull—but he nonetheless continues to hope and push for a meaningful result once his questioning reaches a resolution. The dragon
rebuff's each of Grendel's questions with a cold, empirical retort.
The dragon refuses to let Grendel slip into what he feels are naïve
emotions. That Gardner made the dragon a money-hoarding miser
is more than a mere nod to a traditional staple of dragon lore: the
dragon values money because its presence is tangible, knowable,
and rational. While the Shaper lures Grendel's mind away to more
abstract thoughts of love, beauty, and art, the dragon incessantly
pushes Grendel toward a clear-eyed, cold-blooded intellectualism.

QUOTATIONS

4. I had become something, as if born again. I had hung between possibilities before, between the cold truths I knew and the heart-sucking conjuring tricks of the Shaper; now that was passed: I was Grendel, Ruiner of Meadhalls, Wrecker of Kings!

But also, as never before, I was alone.

This passage occurs in Chapter 6, just after Grendel has bitten off the head of a Scylding guard, thus marking the beginning of his twelve-year war with Hrothgar's Danes. For Grendel, taking this decisive step in creating his own identity is a liberating, empowering event. However, it is unclear exactly what Grendel has decided. On one hand, we might say that he has finally chosen the side of the "truths" that the dragon has passed down to him. In part, Grendel has decided to punish humans for their infuriatingly naïve belief in the righteousness of their moral systems—systems that Grendel knows have no foundation in any kind of universal moral law. On the other hand, Grendel has also chosen to accept the role the Shaper has set for him, as the humans' ultimate nemesis. When Grendel refers to himself as "Ruiner of Meadhalls, Wrecker of Kings," he replicates the *Beowulf* poet's tendency to use a cluster of titles for a single character. Grendel once wished for the Shaper's vision of an ordered, morally coherent world to be true, even if it meant he had to be the villain. It is difficult to tell, then, whether Grendel is taking the intellectual path the dragon has set out for him or the emotional road the Shaper wants him to follow. Perhaps it is because Grendel has reached only a nominal kind of resolution that he feels so unfulfilled. Furthermore, Grendel feels more alone than before because, with his act of symbolic aggression, he has severed the possibility of ever joining the humans in anything but an antagonistic relationship. He has accepted his role as the son of Cain, which brings him into the world of men while forever keeping him at a distance.

5.   *As you see it it is, while the seeing lasts, dark*
     *nightmare-history, time-as-coffin; but where the water*
     *was rigid there will be fish, and men will survive on*
     *their flesh till spring. It's coming, my brother. . . .*
     *Though you murder the world, transmogrify life into I*
     *and it, strong searching roots will crack your cave and*
     *rain will cleanse it: The world will burn green, sperm*
     *build again.*

These are among the first words Beowulf says to Grendel as they
engage in their fatal battle in Chapter 12. Beowulf denounces the
nihilism the dragon espouses while accepting the dragon's basic
premise that time is essentially a "coffin," containing the promise of
death and destruction for all. However, Beowulf also paints an
image of spring emerging from winter, stressing the equal importance of rebirth in the grand scheme of life. This imagery echoes the
song sung at the Shaper's funeral, which also sees the surfacing of
spring as a time for violence and death as well as a new beginning.
This conception of the seasons as a natural cycle full of meaning and
import directly contradicts Grendel's earliest thoughts about the
seasons, which regarded their effect on the dumb ram's instincts as
pointless and mechanical routine.
   The imagery in this passage describes several rigid, hard objects
being burst open with violent but cleansing force. This image is soon
replicated rather gruesomely with Grendel's own head, which
Beowulf is about to smash against the walls of the meadhall. The
forces that break through barriers in this passage are natural and
life-giving in their violence—supporting the idea that Beowulf's
merciless treatment of Grendel is, in a sense, a project of salvation.
Beowulf calls Grendel "brother," which not only refers to the Cain
and Abel story, but also manages to bring Grendel much closer to
humankind than his history of enmity has ever allowed for. Furthermore, Beowulf's reference to the fish in the frozen river remind us of
the Christian elements of Beowulf's character, and the fact that we
may see him as a kind of avenging Christ figure.

QUOTATIONS

# KEY FACTS

FULL TITLE
*Grendel*

AUTHOR
John Gardner

TYPE OF WORK
Novel

GENRE
Postmodern novel; prose poem; bildungsroman (novel about the growth of the protagonist)

LANGUAGE
English

TIME AND PLACE WRITTEN
1969–1970; San Francisco

DATE OF FIRST PUBLICATION
1971

PUBLISHER
Knopf

NARRATOR
Grendel

POINT OF VIEW
Grendel narrates in the first person, conveying his inner thoughts and observations; occasionally he narrates from the point of view of another character

TONE
Grendel attempts to maintain a satirical, mocking distance throughout the novel, but often finds himself slipping into an impassioned earnestness

TENSE
Present, but with substantial flashbacks in Chapters 1–8

SETTING (TIME)
The fourth century A.D.

SETTING (PLACE)
Denmark

PROTAGONIST
Grendel

MAJOR CONFLICT
Grendel struggles, within his own mind, to understand his place in a potentially meaningless world

RISING ACTION
Grendel's exposure to the opposing philosophies of the Shaper and the dragon provide him with two options of how to live in a world without inherent meaning or values: he can either try to create and assert his own meaning in the world or resign and accept the fact that such an endeavor is futile.

CLIMAX
By engaging in a full-scale war with the humans, Grendel chooses to create a system of meaning for himself.

FALLING ACTION
Though warfare fulfills Grendel for a time, it soon becomes just as mechanical and empty as anything else. At this point, the only way out of Grendel's trap is death.

THEMES
Art as falsehood; the incompatibility of reason and emotion; the power of stories; the pain of isolation

MOTIFS
The seasons; the zodiac; machinery

SYMBOLS
The bull; the corpse; Hart

FORESHADOWING
The unresponsive ram foreshadows the unresponsive humans; the allusion to the curse of Cain foreshadows the charm of the dragon and the Christian imagery that surrounds Beowulf; the dark presence that Grendel feels in the woods and the snake he mistakes for a vine foreshadow his meeting with the dragon; the onset of winter foreshadows Grendel's death.

# Study Questions & Essay Topics

## Study Questions

1. *How is* Grendel *structured? How does this structure relate to the themes of the novel as a whole?*

*Grendel* traces the final year of Grendel's life, beginning in the spring and ending with Grendel's death in the winter. As a motif in art, the cycle of the seasons—a natural and inevitable journey—traditionally represents a well-patterned cycle of life, moving from birth to death and repeating in an endless loop that is natural and good. Grendel, however, does not accept this understanding of the seasons. At the beginning of the novel, we see a ram frolicking in the spring weather, ready to capitalize on the season's promise of new growth and sexual abandon. Grendel opposes this instinctual obedience to nature's design, because to him it represents a thoughtless, mechanical adherence to a pattern that has no real meaning. He is most upset, however, because he sees the season having a similar effect on him—he cannot help but swim up through the lake and begin attacking humans, simply because his instincts tell him to do so. The endless repetition of the seasons, every year looking much the same as every year before, also frustrates Grendel, who feels trapped by the static and unchanging pattern.

Grendel views the seasons as static because they endlessly repeat themselves in a fashion he sees as mechanical. Other characters in the novel, however, focus on the seasonal cycle's ability to renew itself constantly, thereby continually providing liberation, release, and the possibility of rebirth. Throughout *Grendel*, images of spring cracking through the hardened shell of winter represent just such a phenomenon. Grendel's death falls at just this moment, when the year is ending its period of winter and is about to return to spring. We may read this ending cynically: as winter is a time of death, we may feel that the conventions of literature require Grendel to die in just as mechanical a fashion as anything else. Or we may read this ending more positively, focusing on the season's ability to "crack" Grendel and provide him with a possible salvation. As Grendel dies, he feels joy and terror equally, leaving us with an ambiguous notion that both readings may, in fact, be correct.

2. Grendel *is a work of fiction based on another work of fiction. What is the nature of this relationship, and how does it affect the meaning of* Grendel?

*Grendel* is based on the sixth-century Anglo-Saxon epic poem *Beowulf,* a work in which Grendel is a grotesque, violent monster who terrorizes a small community of Danish warriors. After twelve years of continued aggression, the great Geatish warrior Beowulf comes across the ocean to rid the Danes of the beast. After killing Grendel, Beowulf goes on to defeat both Grendel's mother and, many years later, a great dragon that kills Beowulf as it dies. *Grendel* focuses on Beowulf's battle with Grendel, and in doing so flips the protagonist and antagonist. Gardner greatly expands Grendel's history and alters the monster's characterization to an equal degree. In Gardner's novel, very little separates Grendel from his human counterparts: he has a high level of intelligence, as well as a human capacity for both emotion and philosophy.

*Grendel* is an example of what is termed metafiction—that is, a piece of fiction about another piece of fiction. In the novel, Grendel, the villain of the original poem, spends more time observing and attempting to understand the humans than actually attacking them. In his observations, Grendel questions the value systems set forth in *Beowulf,* a work that takes place in a world governed by a very knowable, unshakable moral code. In *Grendel,* heroism, beauty, patriotism, and political eloquence ultimately provide little solace in a violent, chaotic world. Indeed, *Grendel* portrays a world philosophically opposed to the world of *Beowulf.* Grendel's world is characterized by equal parts futility and helplessness. The fact that the plot of *Beowulf* predetermines all the events of *Grendel* reinforces Grendel's feeling of being trapped. Even though Grendel himself is technically unaware of the *Beowulf* poem, Gardner does prefigure upcoming events in the novel through significant foreshadowing. This foreshadowing is used most prominently to hint at Grendel's imminent encounter with Beowulf. The arrival of the Geats fulfills a vague, unfocused waiting from which Grendel has been suffering for several chapters. When Beowulf eventually manages to kill Grendel, the latter feels a mix of terror and joy, suggesting that part of Grendel has wanted to accept his role in the *Beowulf* epic, even though that role has required him to play the part of the villain.

3. *Why is Grendel attracted to the words of the Shaper? Why is he attracted to the words of the dragon?*

The dragon and the Shaper represent two opposing elements of Grendel's personality. The dragon speaks to Grendel's rational, intellectual side. Though the dragon has, by virtue of his incredible power, a rare insight into the true nature of the world, the basic premise he relays to Grendel is inarguable and understandable even to a "creature of the Dark Ages" such as Grendel. The dragon shows how, against the awesome scope of the entire universe, man and his little world have as much overall impact as a swirl of dust. This assertion supports the vague feelings of futility and helplessness that Grendel has already been experiencing. Moreover, this eminently rational outlook also helps Grendel feel superior to the humans, who make him feel excluded and monstrous. Despite the dragon's teachings, Grendel cannot shake the feeling that something meaningful will come of all his questioning and seemingly pointless suffering. The dragon, meanwhile, keeps trying to get Grendel to resist those feelings, to accept that they are irrational.

The Shaper, on the other hand, feeds these emotional, spiritual yearnings. The Shaper provides Grendel—and the Danes—with models of the world where things happen for definite reasons, and where people ultimately get what they deserve. This concept of a highly ordered, morally coherent world is incredibly seductive to Grendel, because believing in such a world would help alleviate his feelings of isolation and emptiness. However, Grendel's rational side, as fostered by the dragon, prevents Grendel from being able to wholeheartedly accept the Shaper's beautiful words. Grendel has seen enough of the Danes' true history to realize that the Shaper's moral systems are specious. Grendel's emotional and rational sides appear irreconcilable, and indeed, he remains precariously poised between the two positions for most of the novel.

QUESTIONS & ESSAYS

## SUGGESTED ESSAY TOPICS

1.  Why do you think Gardner made the decision to use Grendel as a narrator? How does Grendel's status as a monster affect the way he tells the story?

2.  What is Grendel's attitude toward language? How does it change throughout the novel?

3.  What does Grendel want from Hrothgar and the Danes? Would it ever be possible for Grendel to attain his goal? If so, how?

4.  Choose an astrological sign and follow it through its associated chapter. What is the sign's relevance? What does it come to signify in *Grendel* as a whole?

5.  Trace Gardner's use of "cartoon" imagery throughout *Grendel*. Why is the use of grotesque, exaggerated humor appropriate in the novel?

# Review & Resources

## Quiz

1. For how many years does Grendel's battle with the humans last?

    A. Twelve
    B. Twenty
    C. Thirty
    D. Fifty

2. Who or what is Hart?

    A. The Shaper's real name
    B. Hrothgar's son
    C. Hrothgar's meadhall
    D. Grendel's cave

3. What do the humans think Grendel is when they find him in the tree?

    A. A strange piece of fruit
    B. A bear
    C. A tree spirit
    D. An ape

4. What is the dragon's final piece of advice to Grendel?

    A. Read great works of literature
    B. Learn to meditate
    C. Run away from home
    D. Find gold and sit on it

5. Who is Scyld Shefing?

    A. Grendel's mother
    B. An ancestor of Hrothgar
    C. The author of *Beowulf*
    D. The god of the Danes

6.    What instrument does the Shaper play?

    A.    The harp
    B.    The flute
    C.    The lyre
    D.    The lute

7.    How does Grendel reach the dragon?

    A.    The Shaper's song points him there
    B.    His mother tells him
    C.    He sees the humans going to the dragon
    D.    The darkness pulls him toward it

8.    What type of animal is Grendel observing at the opening of the book?

    A.    A ram
    B.    A bull
    C.    A goat
    D.    A unicorn

9.    Who, according to the Shaper, is Grendel's ancestor?

    A.    Scyld Shefing
    B.    The dragon
    C.    Cain
    D.    Abel

10.   What term does the dragon use to describe the nature of Grendel's relationship to the humans?

    A.    "Brute existent"
    B.    "Natural enemy"
    C.    "Distant kin"
    D.    "Mutual distaste"

11.   What objects does Grendel throw at Unferth in the meadhall?

    A.    Knives
    B.    Apples
    C.    Rocks
    D.    Books

REVIEW & RESOURCES

12. What are Wealtheow's people called?

    A. Vikings
    B. Scyldings
    C. Helmings
    D. Danes

13. How does Hrothgar come to be married to Wealtheow?

    A. Grendel brings her to him
    B. Unferth brings her to him
    C. She is a peace offering from a rival king
    D. She met him through one of his thanes

14. Who is Breca?

    A. Wealtheow's husband before Hrothgar
    B. The Shaper's assistant
    C. The dragon
    D. Beowulf's childhood friend, whom he defeated in a swimming contest

15. Who is the only person seemingly happy about Ork's vision of the Destroyer?

    A. Wealtheow
    B. Grendel
    C. Hrothgar
    D. The fourth priest

16. What does Grendel take "Warovvish" to mean?

    A. "Wear this"
    B. "Beware the fish"
    C. "What I wish"
    D. "Brute existent"

17. What keeps climbing up the cliff, even after Grendel kills it with stones?

    A. The goat
    B. The ram
    C. The dragon
    D. The bull

18. How, in Grendel's estimation, do the Geats appear when they first arrive in Denmark?

    A.    Dead
    B.    Lively
    C.    Friendly
    D.    Boastful

19. Where does Grendel find himself at the very end of the novel?

    A.    In his mother's cave
    B.    At the Shaper's grave
    C.    At the edge of the same cliff as in Chapter 1
    D.    At the tree that trapped him in Chapter 2

20. How, in Grendel's eyes, does Beowulf manage to best him?

    A.    God helps Beowulf
    B.    The dragon has given Beowulf a charm
    C.    It is merely an accident
    D.    Beowulf is smarter than Grendel

21. What does Beowulf force Grendel to do during their final battle?

    A.    Bow down to Hrothgar
    B.    Apologize to the Danes
    C.    Say a prayer
    D.    Make up a song about walls

22. What does Grendel decide when the bull starts attacking him?

    A.    That bulls are just like humans
    B.    That he alone exists
    C.    That he is never leaving the mere again
    D.    That he is going to kill the bull

23. What school of philosophy does Red Horse best embody?

    A.  Anarchism
    B.  Altruism
    C.  Existentialism
    D.  Objectivism

24. Who is plotting to overthrow Hrothgar in a revolution?

    A.  Freawaru
    B.  Hrothulf
    C.  Ingeld
    D.  Hygmod

25. Where do Grendel and his mother live?

    A.  In an underground cave
    B.  In a lake of snakes
    C.  On a mountaintop
    D.  In a tree trunk

## SUGGESTIONS FOR FURTHER READING

BUTTS, LEONARD. *The Novels of John Gardner: Making Life Art as a Moral Process*. Baton Rouge: Louisiana State University Press, 1988.

CHAVKIN, ALLAN, ed. *Conversations with John Gardner*. Jackson: University Press of Mississippi, 1990.

HEANEY, SEAMUS, trans. *Beowulf: A New Verse Translation*. New York: W.W. Norton & Company, 2000.

HENDERSON, JEFF, ed. *Thor's Hammer: Essays on John Gardner*. Conway: University of Central Arkansas Press, 1985.

HOWELL, JOHN M. *Understanding John Gardner*. Columbia: University of South Carolina Press, 1993.

MCWILLIAMS, DEAN. *John Gardner*. Boston: Twayne Publishers, 1990.

MENDEZ-EGLE, BEATRICE, ed. *John Gardner: True Art, Moral Art*. Edinburg, Texas: Pan American University School of the Humanities, 1983.

# SPARKNOTES TEST PREPARATION GUIDES

The SparkNotes team figured it was time to cut standardized tests down to size. We've studied the tests for you, so that SparkNotes test prep guides are:

## Smarter:
Packed with critical-thinking skills and test-taking strategies that will improve your score.

## Better:
Fully up to date, covering all new features of the tests, with study tips on every type of question.

## Faster:
Our books cover exactly what you need to know for the test. No more, no less.

*SparkNotes Guide to the SAT & PSAT*
*SparkNotes Guide to the SAT & PSAT—Deluxe Internet Edition*
*SparkNotes Guide to the ACT*
*SparkNotes Guide to the ACT—Deluxe Internet Edition*
*SparkNotes Guide to the SAT II Writing*
*SparkNotes Guide to the SAT II U.S. History*
*SparkNotes Guide to the SAT II Math Ic*
*SparkNotes Guide to the SAT II Math IIc*
*SparkNotes Guide to the SAT II Biology*
*SparkNotes Guide to the SAT II Physics*

# SparkNotes Study Guides: